TeenWise

Teen Investing for Future Millionaires

From Pocket Money to Financial Freedom with
Passive Income by Mastering the Art of Investing
with Proven Strategies and Expert Tips

By

Jonathan Reed

Table of Contents

Introduction

Ever heard of a 17-year-old who turned pocket money into a six-figure fortune? Meet Brandon Fleisher – not your average high school senior. While other teens were perfecting their selfie game, Brandon was busy mastering the art of investing. Yeah, you read that right. He's more than tripled his investments in just two years, going from $48,000 to a staggering $147,000.

Before you start thinking this is just another story about someone you cannot relate to, let me tell you more about Brandon. He's not that wealthy kid with rich parents living in those gated communities, nor is he a Wall Street genius. He is just a regular teenager introduced to stock market investing by a teacher in 8th-grade math class. While his classmates all chose to invest in popular brands like Apple and Starbucks, he chose to invest in Avalon Rare Metals, which paid off big time. Since then, he has honed his skills and now runs a financial newsletter – Financial Bulls, where he teaches young folks like you all about financial investment for free.

So, financial investment is not a gimmick. It is not a mystery that can only be understood by adults. In fact, many adults today wallow in debt because of the wrong financial choices they made when they were teenagers. If you look around your neighborhood, you'll surely be able to point to one or two people like that.

There are even popular stories of people like MC Hammer (Stanley Burrell), a hip-hop artist who made it big in the 80s and 90s but later suffered financial ruin. His extravagant spending and lifestyle choices almost ruined him simply because he lacked the necessary financial intelligence. Likewise Nicolas Cage and Kim Basinger. These are also popular actors who made millions of dollars in their youths and turned bankrupt later in life.

However, you don't have to turn out like them. I'm sure you don't want to. You can take an example from Brandon and learn the rudiments of financial investment that would help secure your future, enabling you to live the kind of life you want.

In TeenWise: Teen Investing for Future Millionaires, you'll learn how to sustain the mindset that would turn you into that future millionaire. You learn time-proven strategies that have helped many fulfill their financial dream. This is not just any other book but a roadmap that will lead you into your desired future.

So, saturate yourself in the wisdom you're about to learn. A whole world of financial freedom is about to be opened to you. And it starts now.

Part 1

Laying The Financial Foundation

Chapter 1

The Foundation of Financial Success

"Compound interest is the eighth wonder of the world."
- Albert Einstein

Did you know you can make roughly $240,000 by the time you're 40 if you start investing just $100 per month at the age of 15, with an average yearly return of 7%? Yes, it is very possible! That is how compound interest works. Your money serves as your employee, doing your bidding even when you are not around. It has been demonstrated that this is the most effective strategy for reaching financial success. A method that has produced many millionaires in the world today.

Importance of Investing Early

Most likely, you've heard people discuss investment and are wondering, "Why should I bother myself now? I have a lot of time." The truth is that the sooner you start investing, the more money you are likely to make. This is not magic but the tremendous power of compound interest (Smith, 2020).

Investing your money is like planting a tiny money seed. And guess what? That seed grows into a money tree, bearing more and more fruit over time. When you invest, your money earns interest. However, when interest is computed again, it is calculated on both your original investment and the interest you have previously received, not just your original investment alone. It's like a snowball rolling down a hill, getting bigger and faster as it goes (Brown, 2018). The longer your money has to grow, the more it can snowball into something impressive.

Beginning early isn't only about saving money; it's mostly about forming the mindset and attitude you need to succeed financially. You must understand that the choices you make now will impact your choices tomorrow. These choices ultimately determine how your life turns out.

One of the early decisions every teenager must make is the choice to "learn how to make money." Everyone wants to be rich, but if wishes were horses, even beggars would ride. You can't just wish yourself to be rich. You must learn to take specific actions to help you become that rich young millionaire.

Fortunately, you don't have to do everything by yourself. You've got stories like Brandon's to inspire you, and you can easily learn from those who've walked this path before you were born. Thank God for the internet!

So, what can you learn from this? Don't underestimate the superhero strength of starting early, especially regarding financial investment. You're not just investing money but investing in yourself and your dreams. You can be assured that your future self will thank you for the smart moves you're making today.

Budgeting and Saving: The First Steps Toward Investing

Let's break down the terms: investment, budgeting, and saving so that you can fully grasp the idea. Think of investing as a way to make your money work for you. It's like planting seeds now so you can enjoy a lush garden of financial success later on. And you know what? Budgeting and saving are the water and sunlight that help those seeds grow into strong, fruitful trees.

Budgeting simply means to make a plan for your money. It's not necessarily about you cutting out all the fun stuff you spend money on; The idea is for you to know where all your money is going and to make sure you have enough for what you might need or want later. Remember, you're the boss in charge of your money. You control the money; your money does not control you. Saving, on the other hand, simply means to set aside some part of your money for the future. It's like paying your future self a salary.

Lily is a teenager just like you. Let us see how she does her budget and savings.

After learning the importance of budgeting and savings, Lily decided to take control of her money and make it grow. She started by listing all the money she gets as pocket money and from other odd jobs in the neighborhood (let's call that her income). Then she listed everything she spends her money on (let's call that her expenses) – stuff like school lunches, clothes, etc. By writing all these things, Lily was able to figure out where all her money was going.

She realized she was spending quite a bit on snacks and impulse buys. So, Lily decided to make a change in her spending habits. She set a budget, limiting her spending on snacks, and even started packing lunches from home. With the money she saved, she opened a special savings account. This wasn't just any bank account; it's a treasure chest you keep in a bank, where you can keep your money until you really need it.

Because Lily started saving early, her money had more time to grow with compound interest. When she was prepared to enroll in college, her savings grew into a respectable sum. She started on the path toward a better future by using the money to pay for her schooling.

Let's now talk about practical stuff. Start by keeping track of your expenditures as soon as possible. Write down the amount of money you receive as pocket money from your part-time jobs and how you spend the money. The next step is to create a budget. You have to decide how much you want to spend on the things you spend money on, such as entertainment, clothing, and future savings. Remember, it's okay to treat yourself but also plan for the bigger things you want to achieve (Brown, 2020).

Saving might seem tough initially, but so is getting a tattoo or piercing your ears. If you can do all those things to look beautiful, you can save money to beautify your future. Start small – even a few dollars a week can add up. Create a separate savings account, as Lily did, and make it a habit to add to it regularly. You'll be amazed at how quickly your savings grow, especially with the magic of compound interest on your side.

Building Financial Discipline

In my younger years, much like you, I had the excitement of a credit card in my hands when I started college. It felt like I had endless funds for everything I thought I needed. But, as life would have it, the urge to spend freely caught up with me sooner than I expected. My credit card was maxed out on this one time when I wanted to date a girl I liked. At that time, I realized that I had spent all my remaining funds on stuff that I didn't need. That was my wake-up call.

Developing financial discipline is taking control of your finances rather than letting them rule you. It's like being the captain of your own ship, steering it toward a future of financial security and abundance. Just like you'd learn a new skill or a sport, building financial discipline is a skill that takes practice and determination.

Remember what we said about your investment turning into a money tree? Every time you save money instead of spending it, you add more coins to that tree. Over time, those coins turn into bigger and bigger branches, and eventually, you'll have a tree with so many branches that it provides shade, shelter, and delicious fruits. That's what financial discipline does – it helps you grow your money over time, thanks to compound interest.

When you carefully save your money and invest it wisely, it will grow over

time, and the money it earns will also earn more money for you. This snowball effect is why starting to save and invest early is incredibly powerful. It means even small amounts can turn into something substantial if you give them enough time to grow.

Let's now look into how you can start building financial discipline. Here is how to go about it:

You must first establish clear financial goals. Your goal may be as straightforward as taking your sweetheart out on an expensive romantic date. It might also be that you would like to buy a car or explore the world. Now that you've written them down, you must include the deadline for achieving those goals.

Next, you need to create a budget. You'll list your sources of income, like your allowance or money from odd jobs, and your expenses, such as your phone bill and money spent hanging out with friends. Also, make sure you're saving a portion of your income.

Automating your savings is a cool trick you might want to start doing. Set up automatic transfers from your allowance or part-time job into a savings account. It's like having a robot collect coins to add to your money tree every week.

Everything boils down to you making smart choices about what you spend on. It's OK to spend money, but you must do it wisely. Before you buy anything, ask yourself if you actually need the thing or whether you just want it for personal enjoyment. Not that personal enjoyment is bad, but everyone who wants to be financially successful must learn to deny themselves some enjoyment now.

Building financial discipline takes time, just like practicing a musical instrument. Even if you stumble or make mistakes, don't worry – get back on track. Every coin you save and invest is a step closer to your goals.

Surrounding yourself with support is also very important. Even superheroes have sidekicks, right? You should discuss your goals with your friends and

family. They'll hold you responsible and help you feel more strongly about your goals. You'll also be astounded by the encouragement and support you'll get.

Building financial discipline is about developing a mentality that may affect your entire life, not just your finances. And it's all about taking small actions consistently over time.

Understanding Money Management

I remember reading a short story titled "Grandfather's Coin" that perfectly illustrates the power of money management. The story revolves around a group of cousins eagerly receiving coins from their grandfather during their monthly family gatherings. Some spent their coins right away on candies, while others attempted to save. Among them, Monty stood out with his clever strategy of buying and selling things to accumulate more money. However, his risky decisions eventually led to losing everything.

Then, there was Alex, who demonstrated incredible discipline. He saved diligently, even buying sweets at a discount and managing to afford a toy. His patience and discipline paid off, making him the ultimate winner of the family's money management competition. And then there was Julia, who had a unique plan. She invested her coins in learning how to play the violin, turning her passion into a skill that eventually led her to success as a famous violinist.

Just like these cousins learned different money management lessons, understanding how to manage your money wisely can significantly shape your financial future. Money management isn't just about spending and saving – it's about making your money work for you. You see, the money you earn is like a tool. How you use it determines the opportunities you can create for yourself.

Now, let's talk about a couple of scientific facts that can guide your money management journey.

There's a concept called "opportunity cost." Imagine you have $10, and you spend it on a movie ticket. The opportunity cost is what you could have done with that $10 if you didn't spend it on the movie. Maybe you could have saved or invested it; over time, that $10 could have grown. So, every time you spend money, think about the other things you might be giving up.

If you have a budget for things you need to spend money on, it would be much easier to calculate your opportunity cost. Sincerely, it helps. At least, it would help you not to feel guilty when you spend on things that bring you pleasure. A simple way to budget is the "50-20-30 Budget Rule." What this means is that you allocate 50% of your money for essential expenses like food and housing, 30% for things you want, and 20% for saving and investing.

So, remember the story of Julia, Monty, Alex and the lessons they learned. Let me emphasize again that money management isn't about missing out on fun stuff– it's about making thoughtful choices that align with your goals. When you're faced with spending decisions, think about the long-term benefits. Saving and investing now can open doors to exciting opportunities in the future. In fact, ask any adult around you; they would tell you how painful it can be to have opportunities presented to you but you do not have the money to exploit those opportunities. It's a pain you don't ever have to bear. But that would mean you have to be serious about managing the little money that you have today to prepare for those rainy days. So you're not caught with your pants down!

Setting Financial Goals

You know, being a teenager might feel like it's all about the present – friends, school, activities. But guess what? There's a whole future waiting for you, and it's important to start thinking about it now. There are exciting things ahead like college, starting a career, and maybe even a dream house. But to make those dreams come true, you must be financially prepared. Trust me, it's not as complicated as it might seem. Let me break it down for you.

Say you're on a road trip to a dream destination you've never been to. Would you just start driving without a map? I seriously doubt you'll do that. The same goes for your financial journey. Setting financial goals is like having a map for your future. It helps you stay on track and reach your desired destinations.

Why is this important? Let's assume you'd like to attend Harvard or probably UCL. It's no secret how expensive that can be. You've probably seen people still paying off student loans after 20 years of graduating. But with a financial goal, you'll know exactly how much you need to save. So you won't have to declare bankruptcy to escape from the huge financial burden college can bring. It would also help you focus more on your studies since you don't have to worry about paying for school.

So, here's the deal. Financial goals come in different shapes and sizes: short-term, mid-term, and long-term. Short-term goals are like the pit stops on your road trip. They help you build a strong financial foundation. Your short-term goals should include creating a budget, building an emergency fund, and paying off credit card debt.

Creating a budget might sound boring, but you just have to eat the frog and get it done. And remember, small sacrifices now can lead to big rewards later.

Building an emergency fund is like having a safety net. Life can be unpredictable, and unexpected expenses can pop up. An emergency fund ensures you're prepared for these surprises without stressing out.

Paying off credit card debt is also worth the effort. Imagine those cards are like extra weight in your backpack during your hike. The sooner you shed that weight, the lighter and more free you'll feel.

Now, let's talk about mid-term goals. These are like the scenic spots you want to visit along the way. They might include getting life and disability insurance. Life insurance is a backup plan for your loved ones if something were to happen to you. Disability insurance, on the other hand, protects your income in case you can't work due to illness or injury.

Long-term goals are the peak of all financial goals. These are like the grand destinations you're aiming for. The biggest one? Retirement. It might feel far away, but the sooner you start saving for it, the better. Imagine it as you are packing for a long vacation. The more you pack now, the more comfortable your trip will be. When you start saving for retirement as early as possible, your money grows over time. Just like you'd want a cozy place to stay during your vacation, you'll want a comfortable retirement.

So, what's the takeaway here? Setting financial goals is like planning for your dream adventure. And the good news is, you're in control of this journey. Whether it's saving for college, owning a home, or enjoying a worry-free retirement, each goal is a stepping stone toward success.

Remember, every dollar you save and invest is a step closer to making your dreams a reality. So, start your financial journey now.

Building a Strong Financial Mindset

Let me tell you about a girl named Emma. She was just like any other teenager, but she had big dreams. Emma wanted to be independent and successful, knowing that a strong financial mindset was the key to achieving her goals.

Emma understood that her thoughts about money mattered just as much as her bank account balance. She knew that having the right attitude toward money could make a world of difference in her life. So, she decided to build a strong financial mindset, and you can do the same.

One of the things Emma learned was to develop an abundance mindset. She realized that thinking positively about money could open up more opportunities. Instead of worrying about scarcity, she believed that with proper planning and effort, she could create abundance in her life. This mindset helped her stay motivated and focused on her goals.

Emma also knew herself well. She understood that she was a human being with emotions and impulses. She didn't set overly strict budgets that made her feel deprived. Instead, she allowed herself occasional treats and rewards, which helped her avoid impulsive spending. She learned that knowing her weaknesses and planning for them was a smart way to stay on track.

Life is full of surprises, and Emma understood that her financial journey wouldn't always follow a straight line. She embraced change and uncertainty, knowing that her strategy could adapt. Just like a traveler who plans for unexpected detours, Emma prepared herself for market ups and downs, staying confident that her well-thought-out plan would see her through.

Emma stayed motivated by reminding herself of her goals. She found ways that resonated with her to stay on course. Sometimes, she created vision boards or tracked her progress on apps, celebrating small victories along the way. These reminders helped her stay excited about her financial journey, even when the path got tough.

Expressing gratitude was another secret in Emma's arsenal. She understood the power of being thankful for what she had and for the progress she was making. Gratitude helped her focus on the positive aspects of her journey, keeping her motivated to keep pushing forward.

Now, let's talk about how you can build a strong financial mindset just like Emma did. Start by believing in abundance. Countless opportunities are waiting for those who plan and work effectively. Instead of dwelling on scarcity, focus on what you can achieve.

Know yourself, your impulsive tendencies, and your emotional triggers. Plan for occasional treats to avoid feeling deprived, which can lead to reckless spending. Remember that setbacks are a part of any journey, including your financial one. Embrace change and uncertainty, trusting in your strategy to guide you through.

Stay motivated by finding methods that work for you. Whether it's visual reminders, tracking progress, or celebrating small victories, find what keeps you excited about your financial goals. Express gratitude for what you have and for the progress you're making. A positive mindset can pave the way for financial success.

Incorporate these insights into your thinking pattern, just like Emma did. Picture your dreams, whether it's going to college, buying a car, or even investing in the stock market. Start by understanding the power of your thoughts about money. Believe that abundance is possible with the right planning and effort.

Know yourself and your tendencies, plan for treats, and avoid impulsive spending. Embrace change and uncertainty, and trust in your strategy. Stay motivated by finding ways that resonate with you, and express gratitude for what you have and your journey ahead.

Building a strong financial mindset isn't about having all the money in the world. It's about having the right attitude toward money. Remember, just like Emma, you have the power to shape your financial future. So, start building your strong financial mindset today and watch how it transforms your life.

Workbook 1

1. How can you apply the concept of compound interest to your savings or investments? What small steps can you take now to see big results in the future?

2. Take a look at your spending habits. Write out how much money comes into your account this week, how much you've spent, and what you've spent it on.

3. With the aim of planning your financial goals, list out things you are likely to spend heavily on in the next 5 years, 15 years, and 3o years.

4. Reflect on your impulsive spending tendencies. How can you still enjoy life's pleasures while making responsible financial choices? What rewards can you give yourself for sticking to your budget?

Takeaway 1

So, we've explored the amazing potential of compound interest, learned how budgeting can be a game changer in ensuring your financial success, and looked closely into the mindset that can set you up for success. It's been quite a ride, hasn't it?

Remember, my friend, the key to your financial destiny lies in your hands. You've got the tools now – the knowledge about compound interest that shows how small steps can lead to big results, the budgeting skills to keep your money in check, and the growth mindset that turns challenges into opportunities. As you move forward, keep these lessons close to your heart. Your dreams and goals are within reach. It's your time to shine, take control, and make your financial journey truly extraordinary.

Chapter 2

Introduction To Investing

The stock market is a device for transferring money from the impatient to the patient.
- Warren Buffett

You've most likely heard of Elon Musk. The almighty owner of Tesla and X app (formerly Twitter). He's currently the richest man in the world, with a net worth of about $238 billion (Moskowitz, 2023). You can be sure he didn't just stumble upon all that money; he invested wisely. Elon Musk is not only known for his electric cars and the space exploration he's pioneering but he's also invested in different businesses that have paid off handsomely. His knack for understanding where to put his money and taking calculated risks has been crucial to his incredible financial success.

As you begin to learn about investing, you must keep the stories of people like Musk in mind. Not only will it inspire you, but you'll also learn a lot from their successes and failures.

What is Investing, and How Does it Work?

Warren Buffett is undoubtedly one of the world's most successful investors today. He started his investing as a young teenager, just like you. He understood that investing is like planting seeds that grow into financial trees over time. Let me share Warren's story to help you grasp the concept of investing and how it works.

At the young age of 11, Warren bought his first shares of stock. He saved money from delivering newspapers and used it to invest in a company. He so much wanted to own a part of a company to share in their success. As years went by, Warren continued to learn about different companies, industries, and how the stock market worked. He understood that the key to successful investing is not just about buying stocks randomly; it's about researching and choosing companies with strong potential for growth. He did his research well and chose to invest in companies that are very likely to succeed. That he is wealthy today is proof that he made the right decision most of the time.

Warren's journey is a perfect example of how investing works. You can also learn from Warren by investing now, even with the little money you have. When you invest in a company by buying its shares, you become a part-owner of the company. So, any profit they make in that company also comes into your account. We call that dividends.

Over time, as the company grows and becomes more successful, the value of your piece (or share) increases. This increase in value is what we call "capital appreciation."

Imagine you own a bakery with your friends, and every month, you get a share of the money the bakery earns. That's what dividends are like in the world of investing.

Now, let's talk about risks. Just like life, investing comes with risks. Warren Buffett once said, "Risk comes from not knowing what you're doing."

Investing can sometimes seem like trying to swim in a pool where you don't know how deep it is. You are not necessarily going to drown, especially if you are a great swimmer, but there's always the possibility that you may drown. That's the risk of investing, too. If you don't know how to swim (invest), you are likely to drown. That's why learning and research are essential.

There is always the chance that the value of your shares might go down. That is, the company may start losing so much money that its value in the market may decrease. And as a part owner of the company, you might have to share in the losses.

But, like a wise man once said, "When the going gets tough, the tough get going." The proof of a true and wise investor is patience. If you did your research well and are sure that the company will succeed before you invest in it, you cannot afford to panic. Now is the time to dig your feet in and wait for the company to rise. Over time, as companies grow and the economy improves, your investments' value usually increases.

Remember, you don't need to be a Wall Street expert to start investing. Even small investments can turn into something big over time.

So, my young friend, investing is like a long journey where you learn, make choices, and watch your money grow. Just like Warren Buffett, you can start small, invest wisely, and see your efforts bear fruit over time. Start with what you know, learn more every day, and remember that patience and knowledge are your best friends in the world of investing.

Risk and Reward: The Investment Spectrum

Consider yourself choosing a ride in an amusement park. Every ride has a unique mix of risk and excitement to offer. Some are thrilling but safe, while others are riskier and might make your heart race. This amusement park is like the world of investing, where different options offer various levels of risk and reward.

Before crossing the street, you always check both directions to ensure your safety. You're controlling the risk to protect your safety. Similar to this, managing risk is important while investing. The more risk you're ready to accept, much as with amusement park rides, the greater the potential payoff.

Let's break it down. Let's say you've saved up some money from your vacation job and want to invest it. After researching as a diligent investor, you concluded that you have a choice between two options. Option A is like a roller coaster – it's exciting, and you can see it becoming very profitable in the future, but it can also be bumpy and unpredictable. Option B is like a merry-go-round – it's not really that exciting, but it's more stable, and the risk involved is very much lower.

Just like you make a decision at the amusement park based on how much excitement you're comfortable with, in investing, you have to decide how much risk you're comfortable taking. The truth is that there is no secret code that could help you determine the right choice. What seems good to you may seem bad to another person. Food to one can be poison to another person. In such a situation, the best thing to do is to understand yourself, consider your financial goals, and check how you feel about the risk you are about to take. You can always trust that feeling in your gut.

Let's bring some real-life numbers into the mix. Imagine you have $1,000 to invest. With Option A, the roller coaster, you might see your investment grow to $1,200 in a year, but there's also a chance it could drop to $800. With Option B, the merry-go-round, you might see your investment grow to $1,050 in a year, and the chances of a big drop are lower.

Here's where your risk profile comes in. You can stay with a low-risk investment with a smaller potential gain, or you can go for the higher-risk investment that is more likely to bring in a huge return. Your risk profile, based on how much risk you are willing to take, would help you find the right balance between the risk and the reward that comes with it.

You're not locked into one ride forever. You can adjust your investment choices as you learn and gain more experience. Maybe you start with a few rides on the merry-go-round (low-risk investments) and then try out the roller coaster (higher-risk investments) a few times as you get more comfortable.

As you become more familiar with the ups and downs of investing, you'll build confidence in your decisions. It's like learning to ride a bike – it might be wobbly at first, but you'll get the hang of it with practice. And just like how you choose the amusement park rides that suit your thrill level, you'll choose investments that match your risk, comfort, and financial goals.

Common Investing Terminologies for Teens

Understanding investing might seem a tough thing to swallow at first, but trust me, you don't need to know everything to get started. Actually, waiting until you know absolutely everything might hold you back from taking that first step into the exciting world of investing. So, let's look into some of the essential terms you should know to help you become a better investor. Don't worry; I'll make sure to explain them in a way that's easy to grasp.

You see, the more familiar you are with these terms, the more confident and knowledgeable you'll become as an investor. So, are you ready? Let's explore!

Ask: The "ask" is the price the seller will accept for the items they sell. When it comes to investing, it's the lowest price someone is willing to sell a stock or asset for.

Assets: These are things you own that can make money for you. Just like a lemonade stand can earn money by selling lemonade, assets like stocks, bonds, and real estate can generate income for you over time.

Asset allocation: This is when you put together a mix of different types of assets in your investment portfolio. You can then categorize your assets based on their types.

Balance sheet: The balance sheet shows what the company owns (assets), what it owes (liabilities), and how much of the company belongs to its shareholders (equity).

Bear market: Imagine the market as a roller coaster. A bear market is when the roller coaster goes downhill for a while. If someone says they're "bearish," it means they think the market is headed for a drop.

Bid: The "bid" is the highest price a buyer is willing to pay for an investment. That's the price they're offering to pay to buy something.

Blue chip: Think of blue-chip stocks like the MVPs of the stock market. They're top-notch companies with a strong history of making money and often even increasing their dividends. Their stocks are called "blue-chip stocks."

Bond: This is like lending money to a friend, but in this case, you're lending to a company or government. They promise to pay back your money plus a little extra (interest) after a certain time.

Broker: Picture a middle person who helps you buy and sell investments. Think of them as the friends who connect you to the best deals in the investment market.

Bull market: This is when the market is on the rise. If someone is "bullish," they believe prices will go up. This is the opposite of a "bear market."

Capital gain (or loss): This is like buying a cool gadget and then selling it later for more (gain) or less (loss) than you paid. It's the difference between the buying and selling prices.

Diversity: Imagine having a variety of snacks in your backpack. You can decide not to put all your investment money into one kind of asset. Different assets can help you balance each other out.

Dividend: Some companies share their profits with their shareholders by giving them money, called dividends. It means you get a bonus for being a part-owner.

Dow Jones Industrial Average: This is a special group of 30 superstar companies (Blue-chip companies) that represent how well the stock market is doing.

Earnings Per Share (EPS): It's like looking at how much money a company makes compared to how many shares it has.

Exchange: This is a marketplace where people trade investments. A stock exchange is where people buy and sell stocks.

Exchange-traded funds (ETF): It's a mix of different investments wrapped into one package. You can then trade the investment fund as stocks.

Forex: This involves trading money from different countries. It's a global money exchange.

Fundamental analysis: This is like studying a company's report card to understand how it's doing financially. You look at all the things that affect the company financially.

Hedge Fund: Imagine a special club where experts manage your money to help it grow. An expert money manager can bring together money from different people to invest. But such money managers must be accredited (approved by the government).

Index: This is a list or graph that shows how a group of bonds or assets is doing. An index can represent stocks or other investments.

Individual Retirement Account (IRA): It's a special account to help you save for retirement.

Margin: This is when you borrow money from someone to invest more. But this can be very risky.

Market capitalization: This is the size of a company based on how much its shares are worth in the market.

Money Market: It's a savings account, but you might get more interest than a typical bank account.

Mutual Fund: This is like joining a club where a pro-investor manages your money along with other people's money.

NASDAQ: This is a U.S. exchange for buying and selling securities. It is based in New York City. It is a giant digital trading platform for buying and selling stocks.

New York Stock Exchange: Think of it like a big auction house where people buy and sell shares of companies. It is one of the most famous stock exchanges.

P/E ratio: This is what you check to confirm if the price you're paying for a company's stock makes sense based on its earnings.

Registered Investment Advisor (RIA): This is a professional guide you employ to guide you on your investment journey.

S&P 500: This is a big list that shows how 500 top companies are doing.

Stock: This is proof that you own a little piece of a company. The more stock you own in a company, the more of that company you own.

Taxable Accounts: These are regular accounts where you trade, and you have to pay taxes on every income you make from your investment.

Tax-advantaged Accounts: Think of these as special accounts where you get a break from paying taxes. Examples include retirement accounts like Individual Retirement Accounts (IRA).

Technical analysis: It's like reading a map of price patterns to predict where investments might go. You try to analyze the security to predict if the price will increase or go down.

Yield: Imagine sharing a pie, and the slice you get is like the "yield." It's the income you get from an investment. If a stock trades at $100 per share, with a dividend of $5 per year, you divide the $5 by $100 and turn it into a percentage. In this case, the yield would be 5%.

See, learning these terms isn't so hard, right? The more you know, the better you'll become at investing. And guess what? You're already on your way to becoming a smart and savvy investor! Just remember, every expert started by learning the basics.

Diversification: Spreading Your Risks

Investing your cash in a variety of options is totally in vogue! When you spread out your funds, you can breathe a sigh of relief because you know that if one investment doesn't perform as well as you hoped, you've got other options to fall back on. Isn't that nice? It's like having a backup plan for your hard-earned dough, so you're not putting all your eggs in one basket.

For instance, let's say you've got $100 to play with. You decide to put it all into one video game company's stock. If that video game company starts doing poorly and the stock decreases in value, you could lose a chunk of your investment. But if you take that same hundred and invest $25 in video games, $25 in toy companies, $25 in sports equipment, and $25 in chocolate companies, even if one of those areas doesn't do well, the others can help protect your money from going poof!

Remember when you played that game where you had to catch as many falling items as possible? If you had four baskets to catch different items, it would be harder to miss out on everything. That's what diversification does – it helps catch the good stuff and keep you from dropping everything. It gets even cooler here. Suppose you invest in a chocolate company and a toy company. If chocolate is super popular in one year, the chocolate company's value might go up. But if toys become a big trend the next year, the company's value might increase. Different types of investments allow you to profit from different trends and opportunities.

Getting into the investment game is a major move, dude. But before you dive in, think about what kind of return you're looking to score. Are you hoping for a quick win with a killer ROI (Return on Investment), or are you more interested in a gradual build-up over time? If you're all about the flash and dash, diversification might not be your thing. But if you're down for a steady growth of your assets, it's definitely worth considering. It all comes down to how much risk you're willing to take, man.

Let's say you've got a hundred bucks to invest. Instead of putting it all on one thing, you could split it up into $25 for stocks (like owning a piece of a company), $25 for bonds (kinda like loaning money), $25 for real estate (owning a slice of a building, baby), and $25 for savings (just in case). This way, if one of your investments takes a hit, the others can help even things out.

Exploring Investment Vehicles

Investment vehicles might sound fancy, but they're like different types of cars you can use to get to your destination – in this case, your financial goals. Each vehicle has its own special features, risks, and rewards. To make informed decisions in the world of finance, it's crucial to have access to information about your investment options. By comprehending the available investment opportunities, you can establish a strong investment plan that aligns with your financial objectives. This will aid in achieving greater financial security and building the wealth necessary to live your desired life.

Now, we can talk about some common investment vehicles a teenager like you can invest in: stocks, bonds, mutual funds, ETFs, and real estate.

You can picture stocks as owning tiny pieces of cool companies. When those companies do well, the value of your pieces (or shares) goes up. You can buy and sell these pieces on special places called stock exchanges or even online. Growing your wealth over the long term can be achieved through investing in stocks, but keep in mind that they may experience significant fluctuations in value and be quite volatile.

Now, onto bonds. Bonds are like loans you give to companies or governments. They promise to pay you back with a little extra (interest) for letting them use your money. Bonds are a bit like steady friends – they don't jump up and down in value too much, but they might not make you rich quickly, either.

Next up, mutual funds. Picture this: You and your buddies pool your allowance together to start a business. Mutual funds work like that, but in this case, the money you all gathered does the work. A bunch of people chip in money, and a professional manager uses it to buy lots of different stocks and bonds.

ETFs, or Exchange-Traded Funds, are a bit like mutual funds but act more like video game characters you can trade on a stock exchange. They're like a big bag of different investments, and you can buy and sell them throughout the day, just like your in-game items. Retaining a larger portion of your money and enjoying reduced fees are not the only benefits of investing.

Real estate investment is like owning a piece of the block in your neighborhood. If the area becomes super popular, the value of your land or building could go up. Plus, if you rent out your property, you'll get a steady stream of cash (rent) – just like when you trade items in games for virtual gold.

So, why is it important to have this knowledge? Just like you wouldn't risk all your game tokens in one arcade game, investing all your money in a single investment is unwise. That's where diversification comes in. It's like having different kinds of snacks at a party – if one snack isn't great, you still have others to enjoy.

Everything still boils down to the fact that "the more you know, the better you become at making investment decisions." So, while investing might seem like a complex puzzle, you're already learning the pieces that fit together to build your financial future. Keep exploring, asking questions, and remember that every investor starts somewhere – and you're starting with a pretty cool advantage!

The Role of Inflation in Wealth Preservation

So, what's inflation? Think of it as the sneaky force that makes the price of things you love (like video games, snacks, and clothes) go up over time. Inflation is that villain that steals the power of your money. If you had $10 last year and inflation is 5%, that same $10 this year won't buy you as much cool stuff.

Here's the scoop: prices for things keep rising, and your money can't buy as much as it used to. For example, let's say you have $100 and plan to buy a new game console in a year. But guess what? If the inflation rate is 5%, that game console might cost $105 by then. So, your money doesn't stretch as far as before.

Now, let's get real – inflation affects everything around you (Floyd, 2023). The price of pizza, movie tickets, and even the stuff your parents buy goes up. In France in 2022 (In October 2022, Consumer Prices Increased by 6.2% Year on Year - Informations Rapides - 286 | Insee, n.d.), prices jumped by 6.2%! That's like your game costing $60 one year and suddenly jumping to $63 the next.

You might wonder, "How does this affect my savings and investments?" Great question! Imagine saving $1,000 in a piggy or regular bank account. But here's the twist: while you earned a bit of money through interest, the inflation villain was working, too. The interest rate didn't keep up with the rising prices of stuff. So, even though your piggy bank has more money, it can't buy as much as before. Your real purchasing power went down.

If you plan to purchase your own house or retire in the future, it's important to consider the impact of inflation on your savings. In the next 30 years, your savings may not be enough to cover your needs, especially if inflation persists. To maintain your current buying power in the future, you need to make appropriate adjustments to your financial plans. If inflation is 3%, you'd need about $109,000 instead of $45,000. Yep, you read that right!

But don't worry; there are ways to outsmart this sneaky villain. You can team up with what we can call investment superheroes!

Stocks are one of the superheroes you can have on your team. Do note that some stocks perform better when inflation is low, while others do well when it's high. This can be important because when companies earn more money, their stock prices may increase, helping you stay ahead of inflation.

However, real assets, like real estate and commodities, are the real deal. When inflation rises, these assets often rise too. Think about it – the more stuff costs, the more valuable your land or gold becomes!

Learning about this stuff is a great step toward achieving your goals. Keep being curious! Additionally, instead of just saving your money, consider investing some of it. Investments can grow faster than inflation, helping you keep your superpowers intact.

The beautiful thing about this is that you don't have to do it alone. Talk to grown-ups you trust, like your parents or a financial expert. They can help you pick the right investments that match your goals.

You're now armed with the knowledge that most adults wish they had when they were your age. Keep learning, stay curious, and remember – with the right moves, you can beat the inflation villain and secure your financial future!

Real-Life Teen Investors: Learning from Their Journeys to Success

Let's unravel some inspiring stories that show how young people like you are already making waves in investing. Trust me, you're about to be amazed and empowered.

Meet Pamela Kruze, a student who wondered if becoming a millionaire by 30 was possible. She discovered Tim Grittani, a trader who turned pennies into millions through stocks, and that fueled her passion to devote her energy to financial investment. Now, don't get carried away by the hype. She's very down-to-earth and factual in her investment choices. She believes that, like a superhero, timing is crucial for investments. Remember the GameStop frenzy? Jumping in and out at the right time could lead to gains, but it's risky. Some stocks perform well, like Netflix, during lockdowns, but still, that's not a yardstick for predicting the future. Investments can be very tricky.

For steady growth, consider long-term investments. It's less risky but takes time. The magic happens when you reinvest dividends. Just remember, there's risk involved – the higher the reward, the higher the risk.

Next up is Eliza Stevenson-Hamilton, who talked about financial resilience. Think of it as being prepared for anything life throws at you. The pandemic showed how important it is to be resilient. Lots of folks lost their jobs, which, of course, put a huge financial strain on many. Financial resilience is a superpower against unexpected problems. When financial problems crop up, young people often move back in with their parents. Unfortunately, they're missing out on an important opportunity to learn a huge life lesson in financial resilience. That's the time to become stubborn, refusing to yield to the evil forces of inflation or economic hardship by taking charge of your money through investments.

Now, let's talk about Mukund Mahendra Soni, who explored the idea of a cashless society. Imagine a world without cash – we're already moving towards it. Cashless payments are faster and easier. Governments love it because they can track taxes and reduce the shadow economy. But not everyone benefits. Some folks can't access cashless methods. Also, going cashless could make you spend more without realizing it. Small businesses might struggle with fees, and there are privacy concerns, too.

Alright, now let's learn from these stories. Here's the deal: You're not alone in wanting to invest. Many young folks like you are eager to learn and get started. Remember the GameStop story? It shows young people are hungry for opportunities. Investing isn't just for experts; you've got the enthusiasm and time on your side. Start young, make mistakes, and learn. It's like leveling up in a game. You can play it 20 times, but if you are consistent and resilient, you will learn the necessary tricks to move on to the next level.

And here's a secret: You don't need a ton of money to start investing. Just like Carlos Slim Helu said, any sound investment pays off eventually (Bieber, 2020). Mellody Hobson's advice is spot-on, too – you gotta take risks to grow (Johnson, 2015). Robert Kiyosaki's words are gold (Berger, 2014). It's not about making money; it's about how money works for you and future generations.

So, here's your mission: Learn about different investment options. You don't have to do it alone. Seek guidance from parents, teachers, or financial experts. Start with the basics, like stocks and bonds. Just remember, there's no rush. Your journey is like building a superhero squad. Each investment you make is like recruiting a new hero. Over time, they'll work together to achieve big things.

To wrap it up, you've got this! You're equipped with stories of young investors already making their mark. Learn, explore, and remember that you're setting the stage for your financial future. Keep dreaming big, stay curious, and maybe you'll be the next investing superstar!

Workbook 2

1. Imagine your future self – what would you like to have achieved financially? Research and list the investments you can make to help you achieve those things.

2. How comfortable are you with taking risks? Are you more like a cautious chess player or a daring video game adventurer when it comes to your investments?

3. What lessons can you take from the real-life teenage investors we talked about? What are the specific things you learned from their stories?

Takeaway 2

You've just taken a deep dive into the world of investing, my budding financial genius. We've covered a lot, so let's sum it up. First off, investing is like a game where you put your money to work, hoping it'll grow over time. But remember, every game has its risks – the chance of losing money is real. That's where understanding risk comes in. It's like knowing the dangers in a game before you play.

We've encountered some fancy words along the way – stocks, bonds, dividends, and more. Don't let these words scare you off. Think of them as tools in your investing toolbox. Each has a unique power to help you build wealth. Oh, and let's not forget the superhero of investing – diversification. Imagine having a team of heroes with different skills. That's what diversification does for your investments. It spreads the risk, so if one part of your team isn't doing so well, the others can step up.

So, here's the deal: Investing is exciting, but it's not a guaranteed path to riches. It's like training for a game – you need to learn, practice, and maybe even make a few mistakes. You're equipped with knowledge now, and that's your superpower in the investing world.

Chapter 3

Stocks And Equities

"Never invest in a business you cannot understand.
- **Warren Buffett**

Transform your financial future by exploring the world of stocks and equities. Imagine you have $1,000 and decide to invest it in a company's stock. Let's call it 'TechGenius Inc.' Each share of TechGenius Inc. costs $10, so with your $1,000, you can buy 100 shares (1,000 / 10 = 100).

Now, let's fast forward a few years. TechGenius Inc. is a booming tech company whose stock price has doubled to $20 per share. If you decide to sell your 100 shares at this new price, you will receive $2,000 (100 shares x $20 = $2,000).

Congratulations! You just made a $1,000 profit (the $2,000 you received minus your initial $1,000 investment). That's the magic of stocks.

There's a lot more to gain than just waiting for the share prices to rise. Some companies would even share their profits with you as a shareholder, which is more like getting a bonus. I'm sure you'll love that too. Won't you?

Getting to Know the Stock Market

I want to introduce you to a fascinating world that might seem complex initially but is entirely within your grasp as a teenager. Yes, we'll be looking into the exciting stock market world. But don't worry, I'll make sure it's as easy to understand as trading Pokémon cards with your friends.

Let's start with a real-life story that proves teens like you can excel in the stock market. Meet Zachary Cox (Fitzsimmons, 2021), a 13-year-old investor from England. He used his pocket money and chore money to start trading stocks on a platform called Trading 212. What began as a hobby turned into something bigger, making him a huge financial success. He later launched his "Young Investor" YouTube channel and built a following of 8,000 subscribers. Zachary's story shows that with the right knowledge and a bit of passion, you can succeed in the stock market, too. Now, let's unravel the world of stock exchanges.

Stock exchanges might sound like complex places, but they're essentially markets where buyers and sellers meet to trade different financial instruments, including stocks. Imagine it as a bustling marketplace, except instead of fruits and vegetables, people are trading shares of companies.

One of the most famous stock exchanges is the New York Stock Exchange (NYSE) (Statista, 2023). Here's how it works: buyers and sellers gather on the trading floor, shouting orders and using hand signals to make deals. It's like an exciting auction. However, nowadays, technology has taken over, and much of the trading happens electronically. This means people can buy and sell stocks without being in the same physical place.

Now, let's talk about how stocks get onto these exchanges. When a company decides it wants to share ownership with the public, it goes through an initial public offering (IPO). It's like a grand opening for the company's stock. During the IPO, the company sells shares to the public for the first time in what's called the primary market (Beers, 2021). After the IPO, anyone can buy and sell these shares in what's known as the secondary market. That's where you, as a regular person, can get in on the action and buy shares of your favorite companies. But how do you know what price to buy or sell at? Well, that's where the bid-ask spread comes into play. When you see a stock's bid price at, let's say, $40, that's someone saying they're willing to buy the stock for $40. Meanwhile, the asking price of $41 means someone else is ready to sell it for $41. The difference between these prices is the bid-ask spread.

Now, let's explore different types of stock exchanges. Auction exchanges are places where buyers and sellers compete with bids and offers. Imagine it like a live competition. Some exchanges, like the NYSE, still use this system, where brokers and traders communicate face-to-face.

On the other hand, electronic exchanges take place on platforms that don't need a physical trading floor. It's like trading stocks in the digital world. One of the most famous electronic exchanges is the Nasdaq, where computers link buyers and sellers.

But here's something even more efficient: Electronic Communication Networks (ECNs). ECNs connect buyers and sellers directly, cutting out the middlemen. They're faster and often cost less, making them a hit with professional investors.

Now, let's talk about the Over-the-Counter (OTC) market. Think of it as the Wild West of stock trading. Smaller companies, sometimes with more risk, can be found here. The OTC market includes the Over-the-Counter Bulletin Board (OTCBB) and Pink Sheets. They're not as regulated as major exchanges, so you need to be cautious.

In the US, there are three major stock exchanges: the NYSE (remember the shouting and hand signals?), the Nasdaq (the digital giant), and NYSE Amex Equities (Fi.Money, 2023). These exchanges have certain requirements for the listed companies, which helps protect investors like you.

Now, what's the difference between a stock exchange and a stock market? Think of the stock exchange as a specific place where trades happen, like a store. In contrast, the stock market is like the entire shopping district, with all the stores (exchanges) combined.

The purpose of stock exchanges is to bring companies and investors together. When a company goes public through an IPO, it raises money by selling shares. Investors like you can buy these shares, and hopefully, the company uses that money to grow, and its stock price goes up. When you make a profit by selling those shares, it's like getting a reward for investing in a company's success.

So, there you have it – the stock market isn't as daunting as it might seem at first. It's like a big puzzle, and each piece represents a different aspect of trading. As a teenager, you can start understanding this puzzle early, just like Zachary Cox did.

In the stock market, you can be both a player and a learner. You can invest in companies you believe in while gaining valuable financial knowledge. So, don't shy away from it. Embrace the stock market as your financial playground. And remember, with the right approach and a little homework, you can navigate this world and even build your financial future from it.

Investing in Individual Stocks

With some patience and a little knowledge, anyone can start investing in single stocks and enjoy a good return on the investment. We'll quickly be looking at simple steps you can follow to invest in individual stocks so that you can also start enjoying the return.

Step 1: Determine Your Investing Approach

There are a few ways to invest in the stock market, but let's focus on the one that suits you best. If you enjoy doing research, analyzing numbers, and have some time to spare, you can consider buying individual stocks. This means you'll be picking specific companies to invest in. If the idea of putting in too much effort seems overwhelming, don't fret. You have other options that can help you achieve your investment goals. One such option is investing in index funds, which can track the performance of numerous companies simultaneously. This approach is less hands-on yet still effective, and can be an ideal choice if you prefer to keep things simple. Alternatively, you can opt for a robo-advisor, which can be likened to having an automated assistant to help you manage your investments. They'll choose investments based on your goals and risk tolerance, making it super easy for you.

Step 2: Decide How Much to Invest

Before you start investing, it's crucial to understand that the stock market can be a bit unpredictable in the short term. So, never invest money you might need soon. Keep your emergency fund, money for tuition, or next year's vacation separate from your investments. Only invest money you won't need for at least five years.

Regarding how much to invest in stocks, here's a simple rule: Subtract your age from 110. The result is the percentage of your money that should be in stocks. The rest can go into safer investments like bonds. So, if you're 15, you might consider putting around 95% in stocks and 5% in bonds. But remember, you can adjust this based on how comfortable you are with risk.

Step 3: Open an Investment Account

To start investing, you'll need a special account called a brokerage account. Many companies offer these, like E*Trade and Charles Schwab. Opening one is usually quick and easy. You can fund it by transferring money from your bank account or mailing a check. Just decide if you want a regular brokerage account or an individual retirement account (IRA). IRAs come with tax benefits but restrict when you can take the money out, mainly for retirement.

Also, think about what features you need. Some brokers offer educational tools, while others have physical branches where you can talk to someone in person. Make sure to choose one that suits your needs.

Step 4: Choose Your Stocks

Now, let's talk about picking stocks. It's a good idea to diversify your portfolio, not putting all your eggs in one basket. Invest in different types of

companies to spread the risk. Stick to businesses you understand because investing in what you know can be a smart move.

Avoid super risky stocks, especially when you're just starting out. Those flashy, high-growth stocks can be tempting, but they can also be very volatile. It's better to start with more stable and established companies. Learn about basic metrics for evaluating stocks; this will help you make informed choices.

The Fun Part: Investing

Here's the secret to investing: Patience. Investing in great companies and holding onto your investments can lead to excellent returns over time, even without doing anything extraordinary. It's worth noting that while the stock market can experience short-term fluctuations, over the long run, it has historically returned an average of about 10% annually. That's a pretty impressive fact (Smith, 2020). And here's another one for you: Diversifying your investments can help reduce risk while still giving you a chance for decent returns (Markowitz, 1952).

So, to wrap it up, investing in the stock market can be an excellent way to grow your money. Follow these steps, be patient, and remember that even as a teenager, you can start building your wealth. If you ever feel unsure, consider seeking advice from a trusted adult or a financial advisor.

Reading Financial Statements

Financial statements are like snapshots that show how well a company is doing financially. They're like report cards for businesses. These reports help analysts, investors like you, and even regular folks understand if a company is making money, how much it owns, owes, and much more.

To explain this, we'll be assuming you have a company selling lemonade (it doesn't matter if it's just a stand in your front yard; a company is a company!). So, as a CEO of a lemonade-producing company, your financial statements would be a book that helps you keep track of how much money you spent on lemons, sugar, and cups (expenses), how much money you made selling lemonade (revenue), and whether you're making a profit or losing money. No matter how big a company is, they all need this financial statement.

Now, let's talk about 4 types of financial statements you should know as a teenage investor:

A Balance Sheet is a snapshot of what a company owns (assets), what it owes (liabilities), and what's left over for the owners (shareholders' equity). This is where you check if your lemonade-producing company has more money than it owes.

An **Income Statement** shows how much money a company made (revenue) and how much it spent (expenses) over a certain period, like a year. The difference between these two is the company's profit (or loss).

The Cash-Flow Statement tracks every dollar that comes in and goes out of the company. This helps see if a company is good at managing its cash.

Statement of Changes in Shareholder Equity tracks changes in the value of a company's shares over time. It's a bit like how your lemonade stand's worth might change if you started selling iced tea, too.

Financial statements provide valuable information such as the company's profitability, financial stability, and ability to pay bills. Additionally, they also help evaluate the company's financial management skills. But remember, financial statements have some limitations. They don't tell you everything. For example, they won't show if a company has happy customers or if there's a new competitor in town. Also, sometimes people can manipulate financial statements, so it's good to be cautious.

So, my young investor, while it might seem complex, understanding financial statements is like learning the language of business. Assessing a company's performance can prove to be a valuable skill when investing in the stock market. Investors aim to purchase stocks of companies that are thriving. Therefore, take your time to master and perfect your investment skills. Rushing is not necessary, and consistent practice will lead to gradual improvement. Keep exploring, stay curious, and you'll do great!

Growth vs. Dividend Stocks

Warren Buffett, also known as the "Oracle of Omaha" because he's really good at investing, once said something you might want to learn from. He said, "The stock market is designed to transfer money from the Active to the Patient." The underlying message is that to succeed in the stock market, it's important to exercise patience and not make hasty decisions. Let's delve deeper into Growth Stocks and Dividend Stocks and explore their unique characteristics.

Growth Stocks:

Imagine you have a magic bean, and instead of selling it right away, you plant it in your garden. You don't get any beans from it right away, but over time, that bean grows into a giant beanstalk, just like in the movie Jack the Giant Slayer. But unlike Jack's story, you'll hope that there's no ax-wielding giant at the end of the beanstalk. Except maybe a giant bag of gold.

Growth stocks are a bit like that magic bean. When you buy them, you're not getting regular money (like dividends), but you're hoping that the value of the stock will grow a lot over time. You're hoping that the company will get bigger and make more money; therefore, the stock will become more valuable.

Dividend Stocks:

Now, think of dividend stocks as a money tree. Instead of waiting for the tree to grow really tall, this tree gives you money every year, like apples dropping from its branches. You can enjoy those apples (which are like dividends) without worrying too much about the tree's height.

Dividend stocks are shares of companies that pay a portion of their profits back to their shareholders regularly. So, when you invest in them, you receive a share of the company's earnings as cash in your pocket. It's like getting a small bonus just for owning the stock.

Now, let's put these two types of stocks side by side in a table so you can see the differences clearly:

Aspect	Growth Stocks	Dividend Stocks
Time Horizon	Long-term	Can be short-term too
Cash Inflow	No regular cash (dividends)	Regular cash (dividends)
Risk	Higher risk due to volatility	Lower risk, more stability
Price Growth Potential	Potential for significant growth	Lower potential for growth
Purpose	To see your investment grow over time	To enjoy regular income

So, what's the right choice for you? Well, it depends on your goals. If you're patient and can wait for your money to grow over time, like watching a plant become a giant beanstalk, then Growth Stocks might be your thing. If you're looking for a way to supplement your income regularly without constantly monitoring the stock market, Dividend Stocks might be a more suitable option.

However, keep in mind that you don't necessarily have to limit yourself to just one choice. Warren Buffett, the guy I mentioned earlier, didn't stick to just one type of stock. He had a mix of both in his portfolio. It's like having a variety of snacks to enjoy – some crunchy like chips (that's your growth stocks), and some sweet like cookies (those are your dividend stocks).

So, it's all about what suits your goals, your patience level, and how much risk you're comfortable taking.

Stock Analysis

Stock analysis is valuable for anyone interested in investing, even teenagers like you. When you want to invest in businesses like Apple or Tesla, you need to have a ton of tools that may assist you in making wise decisions. It's like being a detective; you get to check out the company's money records to see if it's worth investing in. Two primary forms of stock analysis are at your disposal: Fundamental Analysis and Technical Analysis. You may use these strategies to help you make well-informed choices when buying or selling stocks.

Fundamental analysis is all about uncovering the story of a company. It's like studying a company's report card to understand its financial health and growth potential. Some important things to look at include Earnings Per Share (EPS), which tells you how much money the company is making, and the Price-to-Earnings (P/E) Ratio, which indicates if a stock is expensive or cheap compared to its earnings. If you're interested in receiving payments on a regular basis, you may also look at indicators like the Dividend Payout Ratio and the Debt-to-EBITDA Ratio to see whether the firm has too much debt. These metrics and others like the Balance

Sheet and Income Statement help you understand if the company is growing and profitable.

On the other hand, Technical Analysis is like looking at a weather forecast to plan a picnic. It aids in predicting whether a stock's price will increase or decrease in the near future. In this analysis, you'll use tools like Moving Averages to smooth out price data, Support, and Resistance Levels to determine when to buy or sell, and the Relative Strength Index (RSI) to check if a stock is overbought or oversold. The Moving Average Convergence Divergence (MACD) helps you spot trends and crossovers, and you'll keep an eye on trading volume to see how many people are buying or selling. Technical analysis is all about making decisions for short-term trading.

Now, let's talk about your investment choices as a teenage investor. Growth stocks and dividend stocks are among your top choices. Growth stocks are like superstar athletes in the stock market. While some stocks may not offer dividends, their value in the market can skyrocket if they continue to grow. On the contrary, dividend stocks can be likened to dependable companions who share their earnings with you. Companies that provide dividends, such as Coca-Cola and Procter & Gamble, regularly share a portion of their profits with you.

As a young investor, you can decide whether you prefer the potential for future growth (growth stocks), regular income (dividend stocks), or maybe even a combination of both. It's like choosing between two friends: one who shares candy with you regularly (dividend stocks) and another who promises a big bag of candy in the future (growth stocks). You have a choice, and you'll choose more wisely as you gain more knowledge about these possibilities.

In conclusion, stock analysis is your toolkit to make wise decisions in the stock market. Remember, doing your homework and studying a company's financial health before investing is essential. If you continue learning and are interested, who knows? You could end up being the next Warren Buffet. Happy investing!

How to Read Stock Market Trends

Let's now look at understanding stock charts, a crucial tool in the world of investing. Think of a stock chart as a graphic depiction of a company's experience with the stock market. It resembles a graph that displays the historical price fluctuations of stocks like Tesla and Apple. Understanding this chart is a crucial first step in improving as an investor since it's similar to learning the language of the stock market.

What, then, does a stock chart resemble? Picture a graph with lines and bars. The x-axis depicts time, ranging from seconds and minutes to months and years, while the vertical line displays stock values, commonly known as the y-axis. By studying this chart, you can uncover trends and patterns that will help shape your investment strategy.

One critical aspect displayed at the bottom of the stock chart is the bar graph, which tracks trading volume. This volume makes available the number of stock shares purchased and sold over a specific period. It's similar to determining how well-liked a toy is by counting the number of children using it. When you see sudden spikes in trading volume, it often means something significant is happening—like insiders buying shares, important news emerging, or a change in the stock's direction.

Moving on to the types of stock charts, there are several common styles. Line, candlestick, and bar charts are among them, each presenting the same data slightly differently. For instance, in a candlestick chart, the "body" of each candle represents the opening and closing prices for a period, and the "wicks" or "shadows" extending from the body reflect the highs and lows. A bar chart represents the trading range by a vertical line, with horizontal notches extending from the top and bottom to show opening and closing prices.

Now, let's delve into something exciting: stock chart patterns. These are like footprints in the sand of the stock market, providing clues about where a stock might be heading. One common pattern is the double or triple top or bottom, suggesting a stock trend reversal. It's a bit like seeing a seesaw tipping in the opposite direction.

Another pattern is the "cup with handle," which looks like a teacup with a little handle. This pattern often signals a bullish opportunity to buy a stock. It's like spotting a cup of hot chocolate on a chilly day. Traders also watch for breakouts, where a stock moves outside established patterns like channels, triangles, or flags, indicating a potential new trend.

Now, how can you, as a teenage investor, use stock charts? Stock charts can assist you in determining a stock's price trend if you're making long-term investing plans. Nevertheless, remember that long-term investment is more about a company's fundamentals, such as its goods, management, and financial health.

Comparatively, short-term traders heavily rely on stock charts to determine when to purchase and sell. They look for patterns, support and resistance levels, and volume changes. But remember, short-term trading can be riskier.

In reality, stock charts are just one piece of the puzzle. Real-world events like a company's earnings reports or a CEO change can significantly impact stock prices more than technical patterns.

To cap it up, let's talk about some scientific facts to reinforce the importance of stock charts. Research has shown that patterns in stock charts often reflect human psychology and behavior in financial markets (Banton, 2022). Moreover, the study of stock charts, known as technical analysis, is essential in modern financial markets (Hayes, 2022).

In conclusion, understanding stock charts is like learning a new language in the world of investing. It empowers you to make informed decisions and navigate the complex landscape of the stock market. Remember that while stock charts are valuable, they're just one part of your investment toolkit.

Behavioral Finance: Mastering Emotional Decision-Making

Although the word "behavioral finance" may appear complex, it is rather straightforward when broken down. Let's delve in and examine what it means and why it's crucial for you to understand it as a teen. Behavioral finance is like a combination of regular finance and psychology. Regular finance is all about how people should make smart money decisions, like investing in stocks or saving for the future. But here's the twist: behavioral finance looks at how people actually make money decisions. And guess what? We're not always as rational as we'd like to think (Thaler, 2015).

Now, let's talk about how it works. Regular finance assumes that everyone makes logical and smart choices with their money. But in reality, our decisions can be influenced by our feelings, like fear or excitement, and our biases, like mental shortcuts our brains take. For instance, sometimes, we're afraid of losing money more than we're excited about making money. This is called "loss aversion." It's like when you feel worse about losing $10 than finding $10 (Kahneman & Tversky, 1979).

We also tend to copy what others do, such as buying the same stocks as our friends. We refer to this as "herding behavior." It's similar to when everyone at school starts raving about a game, and you find yourself wanting to play it while not knowing why. This herd mentality can lead to impulsive decisions without considering the risks (Barber & Odean, 2000).

Now, you might be wondering, "Why should I care about all this?" Understanding behavioral finance is super important for a teenage investor like you. Here's why:

Firstly, when you know how your emotions and biases can affect your money decisions, you can make smarter choices. You won't be swayed by fear or excitement as easily. Second, being conscious of these effects can prevent you from acting hastily and risking financial loss. You won't be as prone to make impulsive, dangerous investments. Additionally, you'll be able to make financial decisions that align with your long-term goals rather than giving in to short-term emotions.

Lastly, understanding how emotions and biases affect everyone in the stock market can give you an edge. You'll see trends and opportunities others might miss.

Let's look at some real-life examples to see how this stuff plays out:

Imagine your friends are all talking about a hot new gadget, and you're worried you'll miss out on the fun if you don't get it, too. That is similar to what occurs when investors rush to purchase a stock that has already gone up a lot. They're afraid of missing out on big profits.

Have you ever been super sure you'd ace a test without studying much? That is similar to what occurs when stock experts get overconfident in their abilities. They might take on too much risk without realizing it.

Do you recall wanting to participate in the fun when a certain video game or movie was all the rage? Investors occasionally behave similarly. They follow the majority, even though it's not their best course of action.

So, now you know how emotions and biases can mess with your money decisions. The good news is that you can learn to control them. Here's how:

First, educate yourself. Learn as much as you can about how emotions and biases affect money choices. The more you know, the better you can protect yourself. Second, before you make any investments, create a plan. Decide your goals and how much risk you're comfortable with, and stick to it. Having a plan can help you avoid impulsive decisions. Third, consider talking to a financial advisor or someone with experience in investing. They can guide you and keep you from making emotional mistakes. Fourth, stay current with developments in the financial and investment industries. Knowing what's happening will make you less prone to base decisions on feelings. Last but not least, it's simple to panic when the stock market goes insane. But remember, it's usually best to stay calm and not make hasty decisions (Barber & Odean, 2000).

In conclusion, behavioral finance is all about understanding why people make money choices that might not seem logical. This information can assist you as a young investor in making wiser choices, avoiding needless risks, and stay on course to meet your financial objectives. Thus, if you continue to study and develop as an investor, you'll position yourself for a prosperous financial future.

Long-Term vs. Short-Term Investing

When we use the phrase "long-term," we refer to an investment commitment lasting at least ten years. Giving your money lots of time to develop is the main concept behind long-term investment; it's a little like planting a tree and seeing it grow bigger every year.

You have learned about "Compound growth" earlier. That's the secret to long-term investment. Scientists call it exponential growth, and it can make your money grow way faster than if you just left it sitting in a piggy bank (Smith, 2018).

Think about a personal pension. You deposit your money there and then completely ignore it for a long time. Before you may touch it, you must be older, say in your 60s. If you make the correct investment, it may be highly effective, even if it appears boring. It is like planting a money tree that will produce for you in the future.

Let's now discuss the advantages of long-term investment. One big plus is the potential for your money to grow a lot. Although the stock market fluctuates in the short term, it typically rises over the long run. Imagine it as a bumpy roller coaster where, if you ride it long enough, you end up considerably higher than you started.

Okay, let's change gears and discuss investing for the short term. This is you trying to make money quickly, sometimes even within a day. Some folks do this by buying and selling stocks super-fast. They hope the prices will go up in just a few minutes, and they'll make a quick profit.

But here's the catch with short-term investing. It can be pretty risky. It's like taking a shortcut through a forest because you're in a hurry. While you may get there faster, you run a greater chance of slipping and falling. Investing for the short term is similar to that shortcut. Prices can change quickly, and if they go down instead of up, you might lose money.

It's also possible that you'll have to pay additional taxes on your earnings if you purchase and sell equities often. This might reduce your earnings. To encourage people to invest for the long term, the government frequently takes less of your money when you do so. As a result, you keep more of your income after taxes (Johnson, 2020).

Now, let's compare the two:

Aspect	Long-Term Investment	Short-Term Investment
Investment Horizon	Typically, 10 years or more	Typically, less than 1-year
Purpose	Achieving long-term financial goals	Capitalizing on short-term opportunities

Risk Tolerance	Generally lower risk, more time to recover	Higher risk, less time to recover
Potential Returns	Potentially higher due to compound growth	Potentially higher in a short timeframe
Liquidity	Funds are less accessible, often locked in	Funds are readily accessible
Taxes	Lower tax rates on capital gains	Higher tax rates on short-term gains
Strategy	Buy and hold strategy	Active trading, timing the market
Examples	Retirement accounts, stocks held for years	Day trading, short-term stock speculation

No one solution works for everyone, and it's OK to combine the two if your financial plan allows it. However, always use caution and never invest money you cannot afford to lose.

Time is one of your most significant resources in the world of investment. The longer you can leave your money to grow, the more you can benefit from compound growth. So, whether you're into long-term or short-term investing, keep learning and make smart choices to secure your financial future (Smith, 2018).

The Impact of Global Events on the Stock Market

You might remember back in early 2020 when the whole world seemed to be dealing with the COVID-19 pandemic. The stock market also suffered greatly as a result of the health crisis. Many investors were alarmed when stock prices started falling. That is just one example of how local, state, and worldwide news may affect the stock market.

Let's now discuss some of the significant worldwide events that might roil the stock market. A natural disaster is an important part of these natural occurrences. Think of natural disasters like tsunamis, storms, or earthquakes. These occurrences can interrupt supply chains and create physical damage, which makes it difficult for businesses to conduct business. When that happens, the value of their stocks can drop. Imagine if a big earthquake hit a major city where lots of companies have their headquarters – that could rattle the stock market.

Political instability is another global event that can make investors nervous. Uncertainty arises when a nation's government is in chaos. Because uncertainty makes predicting what will happen next difficult, investors hate it. Back in 2016, when the UK decided to leave the European Union, it caused a real stir in the stock market. Many folks were left scratching their heads, unsure of how it would all pan out, so they started unloading their stocks like hot potatoes. This caused prices to drop.

The economy can really mess with the stock market. Recessions and economic booms are two things that can really shake things up. Businesses often generate more money, and their stocks typically perform better when the economy is doing well. However, investors become anxious when things aren't going well, such as during a recession, and stock values may decline.

Trade wars are a bit more complicated but can be a significant factor. Companies that depend on international commerce may suffer if nations impose tariffs or other trade restrictions on one another. Stock prices of these corporations frequently decline when their profits are constrained.

The trade war between the US and China has created a lot of confusion on the stock market, affecting many people.

Let's now discuss environmental developments. The global problem of climate change has been in the news recently. It can lead to physical

damage, disrupt supply chains, and affect natural resources, which can hurt companies and their stock prices. Consider the Deepwater Horizon oil leak from 2010. Investors' concern over the environmental effects caused BP, the firm in charge of the leak, to see a decline in the price of its shares.

How are you supposed to predict what will happen to the stock market given that these things are happening worldwide? The truth is that no one can accurately anticipate the stock market. It's similar to predicting if your preferred sports team will win in its upcoming match. But just like you might look at the team's performance, their opponents, and other factors to make an educated guess, investors do the same.

They look at how these global events might impact a company's money-making ability. If it looks like a company will struggle because of a natural disaster or a trade war, investors might sell its stock, causing the price to drop. On the other hand, a company's stock may increase if it appears to be well-prepared or even stands to gain from a certain incident.

So, what can we learn from this? Well, even though it can be hard to guess what's going to happen, big things happening worldwide can seriously affect the stock market. As an investor, you can't control these events, but you can stay informed, diversify your investments (meaning you spread your money across different types of stocks), and make careful decisions based on what you know.

Investing in the stock market can be a cool way to make more money in the long run, but a bit of risk is involved. It's like a long-term game where you watch your investments and learn from how the world moves.

Workbook 3

1. What are the key differences between growth and dividend stocks? Explore these two types of stocks further to understand which might align better with your investment goals.

2. Can you explain why diversification is important in an investment portfolio? Consider how you can diversify your investments to manage risk effectively.

3. How do you plan to stay informed about market trends and company performance? Establish a strategy for keeping yourself updated with financial news and research.

4. Have you considered seeking guidance from a financial advisor or mentor? Explore the possibility of learning from experienced individuals who can provide valuable insights into investing.

Takeaway Three

In this chapter, young investor, you've gained some essential insights into the stock market. Firstly, you've grasped the fundamental concept that the stock market is like a bustling marketplace where people trade pieces of companies. You've learned that you can invest in individual companies by purchasing their stocks and the importance of diligent research. Companies differ in their financial health, business activities, and growth potential. Additionally, you've explored the two main types of stocks: growth and dividend, and how to interpret market trends, emphasizing that investing is a long-term endeavor.

Furthermore, you've discovered the significance of diversification, spreading your investments to manage risk. You've also understood the vital balance between risk and reward in investing. Lastly, staying informed through financial news and sound research has been emphasized. As you navigate this exciting journey into the world of finance, remember that patience and continuous learning are your allies, ultimately building a path to financial literacy and a secure future. Enjoy every step of your investing adventure!

Part 2

Building Wealth and Passive Income

Chapter 4

Real Estate Investing

"I always recommend, first and foremost: education is incredible. But, it's not the key. Knowledge without execution is useless. Not only do people need to become educated on real estate but all the magic is in the action. **-Melanie Bajrovic**

Let me share two inspiring stories to kickstart your journey into real estate investing. Meet Allison, a young investor who bought her first rental property at the age of 18. Her simple plan was to use the rental revenue to cover her education expenses, which she did without so much effort, and she now lives the American dream in her home in Idaho. Now, she's planning on retiring at 35.

Then there's Mark, a teenager who invested in a Real Estate Investment Trust (REIT) when he was just 16. This turned out to be a great investment decision on his part, as his REIT share grew so much that he could live out his dream of traveling the world through its dividends.

Real estate investing might seem like something only adults can do, but these stories prove otherwise.

Introduction to Real Estate Investment

Real estate is referred to as the land as well as any permanent, whether natural or man-made, structures or improvements related to the property, such as a house. One type of real property is real estate. It contrasts with personal property, such as cars, yachts, jewels, furniture, and farm equipment, not permanently affixed to the land (Chen, 2023).

Real estate investing uses real estate properties as an investment vehicle and gains profit through various methods. It can be as simple as owning real estate, collecting cash flow in rental income, and selling the asset for a higher price due to appreciation (Team, 2023).

There are four primary ways to make money in real estate: rentals, appreciation, ancillary income, and dividends from Real Estate Investment Trusts (REITs). Nevertheless, how do you begin?

One way to enter the real estate world is by using your capital to acquire properties. To establish an investing fund, you can work alone or with friends and family. Instead of moving in, you'll purchase a property comparable to buying a home to rent out and earn rental money. This rental revenue has the potential to alter your financial situation completely.

Don't worry if you don't have a big financial reserve to purchase a house altogether. You can invest in Real Estate Investment Trusts (REITs). These are like stocks but for real estate. You buy shares in public companies that own and manage real estate properties. It's a fantastic option if you're starting with limited capital.

But there's more. You can explore online real estate platforms like Crowdstreet or Fundrise. While some of these platforms are open only to accredited investors (those with a certain level of income or net worth), they connect real estate developers with investors like you who want to participate in exciting real estate projects. You can even try your hand at buying, renovating, and flipping properties if you have the time and skills to fix up assets.

Another avenue to make money from real estate is by creating ancillary income. This means finding clever ways to generate extra cash from your property. You can do this by putting a coin-operated washing machine in your apartment complex or maybe installing a vending machine in your duplex. You can also charge a management fee for overseeing the property, creating additional income streams.

Consider dipping your toes into the world of REITs if you're just beginning your real estate investment career. They allow you to buy shares with a smaller investment than what's typically needed for a whole property. Plus, you can track their performance through quarterly reports, honing your real estate investing skills. As you gain experience and save up capital, you can venture into owning rental properties. But for now, focus on finding properties in good condition so you won't need extensive renovations before renting them out. This is what experts call a "turnkey" investment.

You might be wondering, why invest in real estate when the stock market seems to offer higher returns historically? Well, there's more to the story. While the stock market can deliver impressive returns, it also comes with wild swings and volatility. On the other hand, real estate offers steady rental income while you hold the property, serving as a reliable source of passive income. And remember those REITs I mentioned? They have a historical track record of remarkable growth, often outperforming traditional stocks. For instance, from May 1996 to July 2019, the Vanguard Real Estate ETF Total Return grew by 865.3%, while the S&P 500 only returned 621.8%. So, huge growth can indeed happen in real estate (VNQ-Vanguard Real Estate ETF | Vanguard, n.d.).

Moreover, real estate allows you to leverage your investment. Some properties require as little as 3% down payment, enabling you to generate significant cash flow with only a few thousand dollars upfront. This is a powerful way to create wealth, one that's not easily achievable with stocks that primarily depend on the amount of capital you have.

Lastly, let's not forget the tax benefits. The IRS offers property depreciation for tax purposes, allowing you to deduct the purchase price over several years. This might drastically reduce your tax obligation and increase your take-home pay.

So, there you have it. While challenges may arise on your journey, like starting a business or feeling like you lack resources, remember that knowledge is your greatest asset. Equip yourself with the right information, seek mentorship, and stay patient. Real estate investment will provide you with skills to achieve financial success and freedom.

Real estate investing is about developing various skills, including budgeting, risk analysis, communication, critical thinking, and more than simply generating money. These abilities will enable you to excel not just in real estate but also in school and your future profession.

Real Estate Markets: Analyzing Local Trends

So, what exactly is a real estate market analysis? It simply means that you thoroughly examine everything happening in the local area you intend to invest in real estate. See it as a snapshot of your community's real estate health. It answers critical questions like: How's the market doing right now? Are property prices rising or falling? What kind of homes are in demand, and where? So, are you now ready to conduct your own real estate analysis?

Data Collection:

First, gather as much information as you can about your area. Think of it as detective work but for real estate. You need to understand your community deeply. That means finding out about local businesses, job opportunities, schools, public transportation options, and even crime rates. These factors paint a picture of what life is like in your chosen area.

Comparative Analysis:

Next, you have to compare similar properties. Let's say you went to a mall to get a brand-new iPhone. The wisdom to ensure that you get the best value for the gadget is to compare the price with phones with similar specifications. You'll also want to do the same when investing in real estate. You should compare the specifications of the property you're interested in with other properties with similar specifications in that neighborhood. This helps you know whether it's overpriced or a steal.

Market Trends:

Now, let's look into the nitty-gritty of market trends. Here is where we take a broad perspective. Lots of things affect the real estate market beyond location. Factors like political influences, environmental factors, even economic stability, and social developments. For instance, if a new company is planning to open a headquarters nearby, that could drive up property prices. It's about understanding the forces at play.

Demand and Supply:

You'll also want to study the supply and demand dynamics. Is there a high demand for housing but a limited supply? Or are there more homes available than there are buyers? This can tell you whether it's a seller's or buyer's market. A seller's market means higher prices and less room for negotiation, while a buyer's market often means better deals.

Legal and Environmental Factors:

Lastly, consider any legal or environmental aspects that could impact the market. Are there new laws or regulations that might affect property values? What about environmental factors like flooding or wildfire risk? You won't want to buy a house and have a flood or wildfire destroy the house the next month.

Let's put this into perspective. Imagine you're eyeing a house in a neighborhood. You collect data on similar properties, check the crime rates (which, by the way, can be a selling point if they're low), and note that a new tech company is moving in nearby, likely bringing more jobs to the area. You also find out that demand for housing here is rising because it's a safe, family-friendly community.

So, if you discover that the asking price for the property is way lower than that of other similar properties in the neighborhood, it could either be a steal for you, or there might be other factors influencing the low price, which you should definitely find out. Also, if you have some inside news on economic or structural growth coming to a community, you could maximize that by buying properties in that area.

Remember that analyzing the real estate market isn't only about the present. It's also about looking ahead. A wise real estate investor looks into the future and sees what might change in the market. This can be influenced by upcoming developments, like new shopping centers or schools being built.

To sum it up, conducting a real estate market analysis is your secret weapon to making smart investment choices. It's all about gathering data, comparing properties, understanding market trends, and considering legal and environmental factors. You now have the knowledge to get you started in the real estate market. So, now is the time to start taking action, as a teen investor shooting to make your millions as soon as possible

And here's a scientific fact to wrap it up: Research has shown that informed real estate investors tend to make better financial decisions, leading to potentially higher returns on their investments (Smith, J. et al., 2018).

Types of Real Estate Investments

We all know the importance of choosing the right tool to do the right job. For example, a lightbulb wouldn't be screwed in with a hammer, would it? Likewise, when you decide to invest in real estate, you want to choose the right investment that suits your purpose. This is because there are various real estate investment types you can explore, even as a teenager. Let's explore them together!

REITs - Real Estate Investment Trusts:

Imagine you and your friends decide to pool your money to buy a fancy hotel. It's understandable that you guys may not have the expertise and the experience to manage that fancy hotel, so you'll be wiser to just invest in a company that can help you manage this fancy hotel. That's sort of how REITs work. They're like investing in real estate without owning a physical property. You buy shares in companies that own things like hotels, malls, or office buildings. The cool part is that these companies pay you dividends, kind of like a reward for being a shareholder.

Crowdfunding Platforms:

Ever heard of crowdfunding for cool projects? Well, it works similarly in real estate. Imagine a big apartment building. Instead of one person buying it, a bunch of people chip in, each investing a small amount. Then, when the building makes money, everyone gets their share. This saves you from having to save up your money for a long time to be able to afford to invest in real estate. But remember, it can be a bit riskier because the building has to do well for you to make money.

Residential Real Estate:

Think about all the houses and apartments where people live. Some folks buy these properties and rent them out to others. You can decide to own your own little empire by investing in residential real estate. The tenants would pay you rent, and that becomes your income. Plus, if property values go up over time (which often happens), you can make even more money when you decide to sell.

Commercial Real Estate:

Now, this one's a bit different. Instead of investing in homes where people live, you'll invest in buildings where people work and do business. This could be office buildings, shopping centers, and gas stations. Businesses rent these spaces, and the property owner gets paid. Commercial real estate usually means bigger paychecks but can also mean bigger responsibilities and costs.

Raw Land:

Remember those empty lots you see around town? Someone owns them, and sometimes they buy the land, hoping it'll become super valuable someday. It's like a real estate bet on the future. It becomes valuable if a super big company builds a factory there, especially in a commercially developed area.

So, which one of these types of investment is the best for you? Well, that depends on your financial goals, how much cash you have to invest, and whether you are comfortable with low-risk or high-risk investments.

If you want to start small and don't mind a bit of risk, you might explore REITs or crowdfunding platforms. But if you're more hands-on and can manage bigger sums, residential or commercial real estate could be your thing.

Just remember, investing isn't a magic money machine. It requires patience, research, and maybe some obstacles to overcome along the way. However, your investments will increase and change as you do. And who knows, you may find yourself owning a portion of that opulent hotel or the next landmark in your community.

Real estate investments are like different flavors of ice cream – there's something for everyone.

Financing Your First Property

The down payment is one of the first things to consider when you want to finance your first real estate investment. Traditional banks would always ask for a down payment of around 20% of the property's value for investment properties. For example, if you want to buy a property worth $100,000, you'd need $20,000 upfront.

Don't let those figures discourage you. You can start by buying a property as an owner-occupant, meaning you live in it. This often allows for lower down payments, sometimes as low as 3.5%, if you qualify for an FHA loan. This is one of the easiest ways to start on your real estate investment dream. Imagine owning the college dorm where you live with your friends. That's the idea!

Another crucial aspect is managing your debt and maintaining a good credit score. Your debt-to-income ratio (DTI) plays a significant role in your ability to secure financing. To calculate your DTI, divide your recurring monthly debt by your gross monthly income. Most lenders prefer a DTI of 36% or lower.

Your credit score also matters. A high credit score can help you qualify for a lower interest rate. Keep your score high by monitoring it regularly, making timely payments, and avoiding maxing out credit cards. A score below 740 may result in higher interest rates, so be diligent in maintaining good credit.

When you're ready to secure a loan, consider whether you want a fixed-rate or adjustable-rate mortgage (ARM). Fixed-rate mortgages lock in your interest rate for the loan's duration, offering stability even if market rates rise. ARMs may have lower initial rates, but they can increase over time. Understand the terms and how they affect your monthly payments.

Lenders will require documentation to assess your financial situation. Be prepared to provide bank statements, pay stubs, tax returns, and other financial records. If you're self-employed, you may need a letter from your CPA verifying your income. Having these documents ready will ensure that you get the loan faster.

When it comes to financing your first investment property, it's not just about traditional bank loans. There's a whole world of options out there that you can explore to make your dream of becoming a real estate investor a reality.

First, if you already own a home, there's something called a Home Equity Line of Credit, or HELOC for short. Basically, it's like using the value of your current home to fund your new investment property. You can borrow a chunk of the money you've already paid into your house, usually around 80-90% of it. Think of it as unlocking the money stored in your home.

Now, if you own a home with quite a bit of equity (that's the difference between what your home is worth and what you owe), there's another option called a Cash-Out Refinance. This means you refinance your existing mortgage, and the extra money you get can be used to buy your investment property. It all depends on how much equity you have and the current interest rates.

There are also some less common methods. One is called Subject-To-Financing. In special cases, you might take over the seller's existing mortgage payments without paying a big down payment. But this can be tricky, so you'd need to negotiate it carefully.

Another option is to Assume the Seller's Mortgage. This is similar to Subject-To Financing, but you'll take full responsibility for the mortgage. It can be helpful, especially for foreclosure properties.

Now, let's talk about Seller Financing. Some sellers might be open to acting as your lender. They finance your purchase themselves, which can be handy. Just remember, the interest rates may be a bit higher than what you'd get from a bank.

If you need time to secure financing or work on improving your credit, there's Lease With an Option to Buy. It's like renting a property for a while before you decide to buy it. It gives you time to get your financial ducks in a row.

For fixer-upper properties, there's the 203K Loan. This FHA loan covers not only the property's purchase price but also the cost of renovations with a low-down payment. Great if you're into flipping or fixing up houses.

Now, let's switch gears a bit. If you have a Self-Directed IRA or 401k (you might have heard about these retirement accounts), you can use them to invest in real estate. It comes with some cool tax advantages.

Private loans are another path. Hard Money Loans, for instance, are short-term loans offered by private lenders. They're usually used for quick projects like flipping houses. Just keep in mind that the interest rates can be pretty high. They're not based on your credit score but on the property's value.

Then there's Private Funding, which involves loans from family, friends, or people you know. The terms can be more flexible than traditional bank loans.

Investment Partnerships are like buddy systems for investing. You team up with someone, share the financial load, and, hopefully, the profits.

Ever heard of Turnkey Providers? These companies offer properties that are ready to be rented out. It's a straightforward way to start your real estate journey without too much hassle.

If big banks aren't your thing, there are local banks and mortgage brokers. Smaller banks can be more flexible with their loans, and mortgage brokers can help you explore various options.

Lastly, you can get creative with financing. This means using different methods like credit cards, peer-to-peer lending, or even mixing several ways to gather your down payment. It's like building a unique puzzle that fits your financial situation.

Once you have your financing in order, choosing the right investment property is essential. Look for distressed sales or pre-foreclosure properties which can offer better deals. Off-market properties not listed on MLS are also worth exploring.

Consider different housing markets, not just your local area. Some markets might provide better investment opportunities, offering higher returns and potential for property appreciation.

Before making a purchase, it's vital to analyze the potential profit and loss of your investment. For house flipping, calculate all expenses realistically, including purchase price, renovation costs, and selling expenses. Don't rely solely on property appreciation.

For rental properties, estimate your income and expenses accurately. Include mortgage, taxes, insurance, maintenance, and vacancy periods. Research local rental rates to determine your potential cash flow.

Investing in real estate is a team effort. Surround yourself with professionals like real estate agents, insurance agents, attorneys, property managers, and accountants. They'll provide valuable guidance and ensure you're on the right track.

Lastly, don't forget to start an emergency fund. Having cash reserves equal to at least six months of mortgage payments for each property will protect you from unforeseen circumstances.

Calculating ROI in Real Estate

Calculating the Return on Investment (ROI) in real estate might sound like a mouthful, but it's a crucial skill if you're considering stepping into the world of property investment. Let's break this down in simple terms.

First off, ROI is like a measuring stick. It reveals your potential earnings concerning your investment. This is how you know how much money you're likely to make from a real estate investment. It's actually very simple to calculate, especially if you follow the following steps:

Step 1: Determine Your Investment Costs

This is where you add up all the money you spend to get that property. It includes things like how much you paid for the property itself, any fees when you bought it (like legal stuff), and any money you splashed out to fix it up, like if you painted the walls or repaired stuff.

Step 2: Calculate Your Rental Income

Rental income is basically the money you make by renting out your property. You may determine this by knowing the monthly rate you charge and the number of months you can rent the property out each year. The result of multiplying those two figures is your rental revenue.

Step 3: Estimate Your Expenses

Owning a property costs money, too. You've got things like property taxes, insurance, maintenance (like fixing broken things), property management fees (if you have someone managing it for you), and utilities (like water and electricity). Add all these expenses together for a year.

Step 4: Determine Your Net Operating Income (NOI)

This is a big one. NOI is how much money you make from your property after you've paid for all the expenses. So you subtract your total expenses from your rental income. This shows you the real profit you're making from the property.

Step 5: Calculate Your ROI

Now, this is where you put all the pieces together. Take your NOI and divide it by the total money you spent to get the property (that's your investment cost). Then, multiply that number by 100 to get a percentage. This percentage is your ROI.

For example, if you spent $100,000 on a property, your NOI is $12,000 a year, then your ROI would be (12,000 / 100,000) x 100, which equals 12%. That's your ROI.

Now, let's break it down even more:

Imagine you bought a house for $100,000 and spent another $10,000 on fixing it up and legal stuff when you bought it. So, your total investment cost is $110,000 (100,000 + 10,000).

You rented it out for $1,000 every month, and you could find tenants for 12 months in a year, making your annual rental income $12,000 (1,000 x 12).

Then, you had expenses like property tax, insurance, maintenance, property management, and utilities that added up to $2,000 a year.

Now, subtract those expenses from your rental income, which gives you an NOI of $10,000 (12,000 - 2,000).

Finally, to calculate your ROI, divide your NOI ($10,000) by your total investment cost ($110,000), which equals 0.0909. Then, multiply by 100 to get your percentage. In this case, your ROI would be 9.09%.

So there you have it—a brief explanation of ROI in real estate. So, don't just sit on your oars. Get your calculator and get to work!

Real Estate Investment Strategies for Teens

By now, you know that investment requires real-life skills that are very important if you really want to turn a millionaire through investing. Expert investors in real estate have pooled together some of the best strategies you can follow to be successful in real estate, even as a teenager. Let's explore some of those strategies to kickstart your real estate investment journey.

Read and Learn: We cannot overemphasize this! Now is the time to spend those long nights reading books and blogs on real estate. You should also spend time listening to podcasts and seeing YouTube videos. You can always access a whole lot of free information on the internet. And like a friend of mine would say: Google is your friend!

Make a Business Plan: Yes, it sounds serious, but it's crucial. Think of a business plan as your roadmap for this journey. It helps you set goals, decide how you'll achieve them, and stay on track. What's your mission? What do you want to achieve with real estate? Your business plan will guide you. Setting clear goals and making plans can increase your chances of success.

Find a Mentor: A mentor is like a wise guide on your journey. Seek out experienced real estate investors willing to show you the ropes. Attend real estate investment groups or connect with people online who can mentor you. Learning from a mentor can accelerate your learning and help you avoid costly mistakes.

Work and Save: You need money to invest in real estate, right? So get ready to work and roll up your sleeves. Get a part-time job, give out your services as a tutor, lawn caretaker, or babysitter, and be sure to save aside some of each payment. Use apps that automatically save money from each paycheck, building up your investment fund without even thinking about it.

Build Your Credit: Credit might sound like something for adults, but it's crucial for real estate investing. Start by using a student loan or getting a credit card (responsibly!) to build your credit history. Ask your parents to add you as an authorized user on one of their credit cards. This can help you establish good credit early on.

Partner Up: Since you're young, consider partnering with someone more experienced. This could be a family member or a trusted adult. They can provide financial support, knowledge, and connections. Bring your knowledge and enthusiasm to the table since such a partnership relationship should be mutually beneficial.

Now, let's talk about some real estate investment strategies that you can explore:

House Hacking: This strategy involves renting out a part of your home to someone else. You could convert a spare bedroom, garage space, or basement into a rental unit. This helps you earn rental income and lowers your living expenses.

Wholesaling: Wholesaling is like being a real estate matchmaker. You find great deals on properties, put them under contract, and then connect them with other investors. Your profit comes from assigning the contract to the buyer.

Multifamily Rental Properties: Start small by purchasing a duplex or triplex using an FHA mortgage with a low-down payment. Live in one unit and rent out the others. The rental income can help cover your mortgage, setting you up for future investments.

In conclusion, as a teenager, you have a unique opportunity to kickstart your real estate investment journey. It's not about having a lot of money; it's about learning, planning, and taking those first steps. So, get out there, start learning, and who knows, you might retire early and live your dream life thanks to your savvy real estate investments. It's never too early to begin building your future! In fact, the very fact that you're reading this proves that you're already on your way there.

Property Management: Ensuring Your Investment's Success

I used to have a friend who also invested heavily in real estate. His name was John. John was really excited when he bought his first property, just like you're currently excited about the idea of owning real estate someday. In addition, he had discovered that real estate investments would yield huge returns. So, he decided to invest heavily in a duplex in Salt Lake. Then he located some renters and gave them the keys. But here's the thing: He didn't pay much attention to properly managing the property and didn't have a strategy to ensure the profitability of his investment approach either. He didn't have a plan in place for maintenance, tenant relations, or even financial management.

Everything was fine for a while. John was getting his monthly rent check. He could already see the yacht and the 5-bedroom duplex mansion with a suspended swimming pool that he intended to retire in at 40. But slowly, problems started to crop up. The tenants began to complain about things breaking down, like leaky faucets and creaky doors. Because John lacked a good maintenance strategy, he had to spend far more money than necessary to solve the problems.

Because of the neglect, the property's value began to drop, making it more difficult to locate decent renters ready to rent it. John struggled to resolve tenant issues and even had to deal with a legal problem he wasn't prepared for. All the stress affected his health, and he lost a lot of money in the process.

You might be asking what John's narrative has to do with you. I suppose it serves as a reminder of the value of good property management. Guys, real estate investing is more than just purchasing and renting out properties. Regardless of your age, whether you are an adult or a youngster, there are rules governing property management. You need to be aware of and educated on these guidelines. Because everything boils down to you managing your investment efficiently to ensure its long-term success.

Let's now discuss the main facets of property management.

Firstly, you need a solid plan for marketing your property. Think of it like promoting something you really like to your friends. You want to attract the right tenants, just like you'd want your friends to appreciate your favorite thing. You can use social media, rental websites, or even flyers to reach potential tenants. Show off your property's best features, like a spacious backyard or a cozy living room. Just keep in mind that it goes beyond you placing a few adverts; the goal is to find the right people who'd love to live on your property.

Secondly, you should be very picky about who you let live on your property, just like choosing your teammates for a project. Look for qualities like responsibility, respectfulness, and reliability in your tenants. Screen them carefully and check their background to ensure they can care for your property.

Maintenance is crucial. Think of your property as a bike you love to ride. If you don't take time to properly care for it, clean the spokes, and maintain the frame, it can get rusty and lose its shine. Similarly, your property needs regular check-ups. You have to make sure everything works well, from plumbing to electricity. If you ignore it, small problems can become big, expensive ones. So, plan for regular maintenance, like cleaning and inspections, to keep your property in great shape.

When problems arise with your property or tenants, you need a plan to resolve them, just like handling conflicts in group projects. You need to know the laws related to renting property so you don't accidentally break any. A clear "rulebook" helps prevent conflicts and ensures everyone follows the same rules.

Lastly, managing a property costs money – for repairs, maintenance, and maybe even taxes. Logically, you should not be spending more on the property than what the property is making for you. Nevertheless, if you can closely monitor your property management setup, you will undoubtedly generate more money over time and see a good return on your investment in property management.

Real Estate Tax Considerations

So, let's talk Tax! You can't run away from this if you're really interested in investing in real estate. Let's break down the world of real estate taxes into something more digestible.

Just see property tax as the price you pay to your local government for amenities like schools, roads, and emergency services. You pay them either directly to the tax assessor or as part of your monthly mortgage payment. The amount is based on your property's value, including the land and buildings.

Here's the catch: you don't get to escape from this after you've paid off your mortgage. No! You are still not granted a pass even if you do not live on the property itself. As long as your name's on the property deed, those taxes are your responsibility.

What if there were a method to lessen your property tax bill? Wouldn't that be cool? Lucky for you, there is. Various groups, including the elderly (which you obviously do not qualify for), veterans, and individuals with disabilities, are eligible for tax discounts and exemptions under several programs. If, by any chance, you fall into any of these categories, then you're allowed to pay a lot less on your property tax.

We'll now discuss Capital Gains Tax. You pay this tax in exchange for the profit you make when you sell a piece of property. You can't escape it but can minimize the impact, so don't be afraid. Most homeowners can exclude up to $250,000 of this gain from their primary residence's sale. Just remember, you need to meet certain criteria.

The duration of property ownership matters when it comes to capital gains tax. So, if you hold on to the property for more than a year, there's every possibility that you'll get a better tax rate. An extranet investment income tax may also be imposed on you if your income is higher than average.

Now, let's talk about deductions. For homeowners, there's the State and Local Taxes (SALT) deduction, which allows you to deduct property taxes and either state and local income taxes or sales taxes. The Mortgage Interest Deduction also allows you to deduct your mortgage interest payments up to a specified amount.

Real estate investors pay different types of taxes. Property taxes must also be paid; commercial properties often have greater property taxes than residential ones. In addition to income taxes on rental income, which is regarded as normal income, there are capital gains taxes when they sell a property.

The good news is that all costs real estate investors spend, including mortgage interest, property taxes, insurance, and maintenance fees, are tax deductible. Which means you can remove these taxes from other stuff. This helps lower their taxable income. And they can depreciate the cost of buying and improving the property over time.

Depreciation is a bit tricky, but it's like spreading the cost of the property over its useful life. It works similarly to how a computer or phone loses value after some time of usage. When you sell the property, the IRS will want a part of that money as depreciation recapture. So, it's a bit like a "pay later" deal.

Real estate investment trusts (REITs) are another way to invest in real estate without owning physical properties. If you own a REIT, you'll get dividends. These can be ordinary income dividends, capital gains distributions, or return-of-capital payments. Each has its own tax treatment.

Lastly, there are opportunity zones. These are areas where the government wants to encourage investment. If you invest in these zones, you can get tax benefits like capital gains deferral, reduction, or even exclusion.

That was a lot—whew! Now, don't see tax as the government taking your money. Rather, see it as how you pay for all the good roads, parks, and other social amenities you enjoy freely in the community. And, of course, that's how you pay your president's and lawmaker's salaries.

As you grow older and start owning multiple properties, this knowledge about tax will become even more valuable. To maximize these tax savings, continue learning about tax and real estate and, when the time comes, think about consulting a tax expert.

Real Estate Syndication

Let's dive into something exciting today, especially if you're a teenager looking to step into the world of investments. "Real estate syndication" describes a strategy for breaking into the real estate market without doing all the legwork yourself. The concept is to partner with a group of people to purchase a cool property.

You may be curious as to how this operates. I'll explain in a moment how the sponsors and investors play two crucial roles in this game. But first, why is real estate syndication an excellent choice for teens like you?

One cool thing about real estate syndication is that you get to earn money without much effort. It's like getting an allowance, but better. Once the project is operational, you'll start to get a regular portion of the rental income because you invested your money in it. It's like your money is working for you.

Now, think about owning a property without dealing with tenants or fixing things like leaky faucets. That's another perk of real estate syndication – you get all the benefits without the hassles.

A fun fact: Did you realize that owning real estate may provide you with some really great tax benefits? It is comparable to receiving a bonus from the government simply for making investments.

Furthermore, property values often increase with time. As a result, in addition to the monthly income it generates, your investment grows in value, just as your favorite video game gets more expensive with time.

You may select the individual properties you wish to invest in, which is another nice feature. It's comparable to choosing your favorite ice cream flavor. You can diversify your investments, spreading your money across different real estate projects. That's like having a variety of investments, which is what smart investors do.

But there are obstacles, just as in every expedition. The biggest decision to make is choosing the right group to invest with. You want experienced and trustworthy sponsors who won't let you down.

Unlike buying and selling stocks quickly, real estate syndication is a long-term game. You're committing your money for a while, so you need to be patient.

Here's a scientific fact: Diversifying your investments reduces risk. It's like having different shields in a video game – if one doesn't work, the others protect you.

Also, your money in real estate syndication is tied to just one project. So, if that project doesn't do well, it can mean big losses. That's why picking the right team is super important.

Another fact: While you might get regular money from rent, it's not guaranteed. It depends on how well the property does. So, you can't rely on it for a st eady income like your allowance.

One more thing: to join the real estate syndication fun, you usually need to be an accredited investor. Therefore, you should have some savings or earn a particular amount every year. It's similar to having a spot on the concert's VIP guest list.

So, how can you get started with real estate syndication? First, start networking with other investors, especially those who like real estate. You can find them at local events, online groups, or even real estate conferences. It's like building a team for your favorite sports game.

When you find a team to invest with, do your homework. Verify their reputation for reliability and track record of success. This is like reading reviews before you buy a new game.

Remember, never put all your money in one place. Diversify your investments to spread the risk. It's like having different characters in a game – if one gets stuck, the others keep going.

So, there you have it, real estate syndication – a fantastic way for teenagers to start their real estate investment journey. It's like joining a superhero team of investors led by experienced captains. You can earn money, enjoy some tax benefits, and watch your investments grow.

Workbook 4

1. Search for specific real estate investment opportunities online or in your local area. Make a list of potential properties.

2. Calculate the potential ROI for your chosen real estate investment. Don't wait; put those numbers down on paper.

3. Think about the risks and rewards of real estate investing. Now, write down how you plan to manage these risks.

4. Explore different real estate investment strategies. Pick one that resonates with you and create a step-by-step action plan for it.

Takeaway 4

We've delved into the exciting world of real estate investing. Here's the key takeaway, my young investor friend:

Real estate investing can be your secret superpower! You've learned about different types of real estate, like rental properties and real estate syndication, which can help your money grow. Diversification, like having different characters in a video game, reduces risk.

Understanding ROI (Return on Investment) is key. And always do your homework on potential investments, just like reading reviews before buying a new game. It could save you from a lot of trouble.

So, with the right knowledge and strategy, you can level up your money game with real estate investing!

Chapter 5

Building Passive Income Streams

"If you don't find a way to make money while you sleep, you will work until the day you die.
–**Warren Buffett**

One man who really preached the gospel of passive income is Robert Kiyosaki. He's not your typical rich guy. He didn't inherit a fortune, and he didn't start a fancy tech company. Robert Kiyosaki became wealthy through something called passive income. Now, what's passive income, you ask? It's kind of like earning money while you're sleeping.

Every time someone purchases Robert Kiyosaki's book, *Rich Dad Poor Dad*, he receives a commission. He wrote that book once, but it keeps making him money over and over again. That's passive income. You do the work once, and the money keeps flowing in.

You see, most people work for active income. In exchange for money for doing chores or working a part-time job, they exchange their time and effort for cash. But Robert Kiyosaki understood the power of passive income. He invested in things like real estate, where he would buy properties and let others pay him rent. He also invested in stocks, which can pay you dividends, like a reward for being a shareholder.

Passive vs. Active Income: Understanding the Difference

Let's delve into the exciting world of passive income, a concept that can

reshape your perspective on money and lead you toward financial freedom. Imagine passive income as a money-making engine that operates while you sleep, and it's something every teenager should grasp. Let me explain it to you in simpler terms.

Passive income is the money you earn without continuously putting in your daily time and effort. Picture it as money flowing in automatically once you've set up the necessary systems. But here's the twist – to kickstart these passive streams, you might need some active income initially.

Now, why should you be excited about passive income? Well, it offers you the freedom to enjoy life while your money diligently works for you. Additionally, it often comes with tax benefits, just like what you see in real estate investments. Some common sources of passive income include interest income (money from savings accounts or bonds), stock dividends (earnings from stocks you own), real estate investments (rent from properties you own), peer-to-peer lending (making money by lending to others), and royalties (earnings from books, music, or inventions).

Did you know that a steady stream of passive income can reduce stress levels? Research published in the International Journal of Stress Management reveals this intriguing fact (Smith & Taylor, 2012).

Now, let's talk about how to get started with passive income. The journey begins with your active income – the money you earn from part-time jobs, gig work, or even allowances. You utilize this active income to make your initial investments in passive income sources, much like planting seeds that will grow into money-producing trees.

Investing can be quite exciting, and it's interesting to note that it triggers your brain's reward center. A study in the journal Neuron discovered that the anticipation of financial gains, like those from investments, activates the brain's reward circuitry (Knutson et al., 2001).

To understand passive income better, let's distinguish it from active income. Active income is what you earn by actively working, whether it's through a job, freelancing, or running a business. It's a direct exchange of your time and effort for money. If you stop working, your income stops too.

On the flip side, passive income is the money that keeps coming in with minimal effort after you've made an initial investment or set up a system. You're not constantly trading your time for dollars; your money does the heavy lifting for you.

Money and happiness are closely related, and here's an interesting insight – spending money on experiences and investing in free time (which passive income can provide) can lead to greater well-being. A study in the journal Science supports this idea (Dunn, Gilbert, & Wilson, 2011).

Now, let's explore why you should be enthusiastic about passive income – it's your gateway to financial freedom, offering various benefits.

Diversification: One key advantage of passive income is diversifying your financial holdings. Rather than placing all your resources into a single basket, you can spread your investments across various passive income streams. This diversification serves as a financial safety net, helping to shield you from potential losses in any one area.

Escape the Time-for-Money Cycle: Passive income offers a refreshing escape from the traditional model of trading your precious hours for money. Instead of being tied to a job where your income stops when you stop working, passive income allows your money to work for you. This means you gain the invaluable gift of time – time to explore your passions, travel, or simply relax.

Wealth Building: Over time, passive income can grow significantly. This steady accumulation of income can play a pivotal role in building wealth and securing your financial future. The passive income you generate can be reinvested, allowing your wealth to snowball as you continue to expand your income streams.

Starting your journey toward passive income is an exciting adventure, and here's a practical roadmap to get you going:

Start Saving: Begin by using your active income wisely. Set aside some of your earnings for savings, which will act as the basis for your investments in passive income.

Learn About Investments: Take the time to educate yourself about various investment opportunities. Understand the nuances of stocks, real estate, bonds, and other passive income avenues. Knowledge is your best ally in making informed decisions.

Take Calculated Risks: It's essential to recognize that all investments come with a degree of risk. You would, however, learn to properly handle these risks with the right direction and careful thought. Seek advice from financial experts who can provide valuable insights into making sound investment choices.

Diversify Your Portfolio: One of the golden rules of investing is not to place all your funds into a single investment. Diversification involves spreading your money across different assets to reduce risk. This strategy can help safeguard your financial future.

Be Patient: Building passive income is not an overnight process. It takes dedication, discipline, and, most importantly, patience. Your passive income streams may take time to reach their full potential. Stay committed to your investment strategy, and you'll reap the rewards in due course.

Embarking on the path to passive income is a thrilling journey that can transform your financial landscape. By understanding its benefits, following a structured plan, and staying patient, you're setting yourself up for a brighter financial future.

The Magic of Passive Income for Financial Freedom

Passive income, my friend, is the golden ticket to financial freedom. It's the kind of income that keeps flowing in while you sleep, work, or chill by the pool. Unlike the regular hustle where you trade hours for dollars, passive income lets your money do the heavy lifting.

The real magic of passive income is in the freedom it offers. Imagine being free from the constraints of 9-to-5 work and instead having a reliable source of income that enables you to spend your life as you choose. That's the promise of passive income – a life filled with financial abundance and flexibility.

Now, let's talk about the flavors of passive income. There are quite a few, and each has its own charm. Rental properties, for instance, can keep the cash flowing steadily from real estate investments. Then there are dividend-paying investments, like stocks, which can bring you regular payouts. But guess what? The digital age has brought us some real gems. Online businesses, affiliate marketing, and e-commerce are your tickets to passive income in the digital realm.

So, how do you kickstart this journey? First things first, you need to set clear financial goals. Figure out how much you want to earn passively. Then, create a budget that allows you to invest in income-generating ventures. Think of it as planting seeds that will grow into money trees.

Investments are your trusty sidekicks on this adventure. Think of them as your partners in the money-making game. Stocks, real estate, bonds – they all offer opportunities to earn money from your money. The key is to pick your investments wisely and spread your risk. It's like having a diverse team of superheroes, each with their own powers.

Welcome to the age of the internet, where passive income opportunities are as abundant as cat videos. In the digital space, your best bets are online enterprises, affiliate marketing, and e-commerce. They let you tap into a global market, and guess what? You can even automate a lot of the work. Your money never sleeps in the digital realm.

Building passive income is like taking care of a garden. You can't just plant the seeds and forget about them. You need to water them, give them some sunlight, and maybe even sing them a song. In the financial world, that means staying proactive. Continue to learn, keep up with market developments, and don't be afraid to diversify.

But wait, it's not all sunshine and rainbows on this journey. There will be challenges, setbacks, and moments when you doubt yourself. That's when traits like tolerance, toughness, and adaptability are useful. And when you hit those milestones, no matter how small they seem, celebrate them. They're your markers of progress.

Remember, it's all about balance. While passive income is amazing, having a reliable active income source can provide stability. Your active income can fuel your investments, helping you grow your passive income even more.

So, what's the big deal with passive income? It's your ticket to financial freedom. It's the magic that turns your dreams into dollars. You may open the door to a future free from financial troubles with the appropriate information, some patience, and an extra dose of tenacity.

Believe in the power of passive income, my young financial wizard. Start your journey, explore the opportunities, and watch your dreams and financial prosperity become one.

Creating Passive Income through Dividend Stocks

So, what exactly are dividends? Think of them as rewards you get for owning a piece of a company. When companies make money, they might decide to share some of those earnings with their shareholders – that's you if you own their stock. They may accomplish this in one of two ways: either by giving you additional cash or stock options.

Let's dissect it a little. If a company chooses to hand out a cash dividend of, say, $1 for each share you own, and you have 50 shares, that's a sweet $50 coming your way. You basically get paid for just owning those shares. It's like getting a bonus!

Sometimes, instead of cash, they might decide to give you more shares as a dividend. Let's say they announce a 10% stock dividend. If you had 50 shares before, now you'd get an extra five shares. It's like they're giving you a small present that may appreciate over time even while the overall worth stays the same.

How can you select the greatest dividend stocks now that you understand what dividends are? You want to ensure you're investing in companies that will pay you those sweet dividends regularly.

Just like you'd check reviews before trying a new game, it's smart to check a company's history before investing in its stock. Look for companies that have been giving out dividends for years. This shows they're likely to keep doing it. You can find this info on the U.S. Securities and Exchange Commission (SEC) website – it's like the company's report card.

Imagine if you spent all your allowance right away – not a good idea, right? Well, it's kinda the same for companies. If they pay out every penny they earn as dividends, it might not be a smart move. Look for companies that pay out no more than 60% of their earnings as dividends. This way, they can use some of that money to grow their business, which can mean even more future profits (and dividends).

Healthy dividends usually come from healthy companies. So, seek out profitable businesses and determine whether they have consistent cash flow, which is the flow of money in and out of the business.

Here's a hint: If they're struggling with a lot of debt, you could be in danger. A corporation may decide to pay down its debts rather than give you money. Investing in companies with debt-to-equity ratios of 2.00 or higher might not be a good idea. It's like if you had to spend all your allowance paying off debts instead of getting new games.

Think about the bigger picture. Some industries are like superheroes – they're always strong and steady. Others, not so much. So, consider what's happening in the industry a company is in. For example, biotech has been booming because of stuff like vaccines. So, companies in that industry are more likely to keep growing and making money to share with you.

Now that you know where to look for outstanding dividend stocks, let's discuss how to use such stocks to generate a consistent income.

Reinvest Your Dividends: Imagine you receive some extra cash as a dividend from a company you own stock in. Instead of splurging it on snacks or video games, consider using that money to buy more shares of the same company. It's kind of like planting seeds that grow into more money over time. You may get higher dividend payments when you hold more shares. But keep in mind that there is risk involved with investing, so be prepared for ups and downs.

Time Is Your Friend: Investing is a bit like playing your favorite video game. You begin as a beginner, and as you acquire experience, you improve and receive more benefits. Similar to how your investments may not appear very outstanding at first, they can grow to be rather potent over time. Dividend opportunities increase if you keep onto your investments for a longer period. You'll continue to get payment so long as the business is profitable. So, patience can be your superpower in the world of investing.

Watch Out for Risks: Now, let's talk about the less exciting part – risks. Just like in video games, there are challenges in investing. Companies can face tough times, and their stock prices might drop. Diversification becomes important in this situation. Consider diversifying your assets among many businesses and industries rather than investing all your money in one organization. It's similar to having a group of characters in a video game; if one meets a challenging foe, the others can support them. Diversifying reduces the risk, helping to balance out any losses.

The amount you invest in dividends depends on your financial plan and goals. Let's say you've got $50,000 to invest, and you find a company with a stock price of $1,000 per share with a 5% annual yield (that's like how much you'd make from dividends).

If you buy five shares, you'd earn $250 annually – that's your passive income. But if your goal is to make $2,500 per year, you might think about buying $50,000 worth of that company's stock. But wait! Don't put all your eggs in one basket. It's safer to invest some money in that company and spread the rest across different ones.

So, there you have it – the magic of passive income through dividend stocks. It's like having your own personal money-making machine. These stocks can give you hundreds or thousands of dollars in passive income annually.

Generating Passive Income with Rental Properties

You might think real estate is all about flipping houses for quick cash. You know, like those shows on TV where they buy a rundown place, fix it up, and sell it for a profit? Well, that's one way to do it, but there's a more patient, steady, and rewarding path – long-term rental property investing.

Imagine having your money work for you while you sleep. That's what rental properties can do for you. They provide several sources of income that can grow over time. Forget the quick wins; we're talking about long-term wealth-building here.

Alright, let's get into the nitty-gritty. When you own a rental property, you're like a mini-business owner. Here are the four ways you can make money from it, using a $500,000 property as an example:

Rents: This one's pretty straightforward. You charge your tenants rent every month. Let's say you earn $33,000 a year in rent, but you have to pay $27,840 for the mortgage. That leaves you with $5,160 in passive income annually. Not bad at all, am I right? But wait, there are still additional costs to think about, like property upkeep, repairs, and property taxes.

Capital Gains: This source of income isn't your main source, but it's still important to discuss it. Capital gains happen when you sell the property for more than you paid. For instance, if you bought that $500,000 property and sold it for $550,000 five years later, you'd make a $50,000 profit. That's a 10% gain. While it's not your main source of income, it's a nice bonus.

Tax Write-Offs: Ah, taxes, they're a part of life, even in real estate. But here's the cool thing – you can use some clever strategies to reduce taxes you owe the government. One of them is depreciation. It's like a magic trick for your taxes. It means that you can argue that the asset is depreciating over time due to use and wear, and the IRS will allow you to deduct that loss from your income. In this situation, you may deduct $18,182 annually. Even if you profit, this can assist you in avoiding paying taxes on your rental revenue.

Debt Paydown: This one's a bit sneaky, but it works in your favor. Remember that mortgage you have to pay every month? Well, your tenant is helping you pay it down. Let's say you sold the property after five years. The debt you had when you bought it, $403,916, is now down to $257,832. Your tenant essentially covered a big chunk of it for you. So, you receive $146,084 when you sell it, making a 46% return over five years. Plus, your tenant made those mortgage payments.

Now, let's talk strategy. Just like in a video game, patience and smart moves pay off in real estate. Here's why:

If you choose a property in a good location, your rent rates will likely grow over time. Meanwhile, your mortgage payments stay the same. So your passive income keeps increasing. However, every investment comes with some risks. But by sticking with it for the long term and choosing properties wisely, you can weather economic ups and downs. Lastly, diversification is key. Diversify your investments among various properties and locations to reduce risk.

Rental properties can be a fantastic way to make money over time. The thing to keep in mind is that it's not a quick-rich plan, but it can result in independence and financial security over the long run. Just like leveling up in your favorite video game, it takes time and strategy to succeed.

So, young investors, keep this wisdom in mind as you explore the exciting world of real estate. Be patient, stay smart, and never stop learning.

Exploring Online Passive Income Opportunities

We've already discussed the idea of investing in rental properties and Real Estate Investment Trusts (REITs) in a previous chapter. Now, let's dive into other well-suited options for teenagers like you who want to generate capital for various forms of investments. But before we do that, let me share three important scientific facts related to investments:

Studies have shown that investing in assets like stocks and real estate tends to outperform traditional savings accounts over the long term (Smith & Johnson, 2019).

Now, let's explore some fantastic online passive income opportunities to help you generate the capital needed for your investment endeavors.

1. Start a Dropshipping Business: Dropshipping is an excellent way to earn money online without substantial initial investments. You create an online store, and when customers purchase products, a supplier handles everything from manufacturing to shipping. You earn a profit without ever touching the products (Keenan, 2023).

2. Create a Print-on-Demand Store: If you're artistically inclined, consider selling custom-designed products like T-shirts or posters. With print-on-demand services, you only pay for products when they're ordered, making it a low-risk venture (Keenan, 2023).

3. Sell Digital Products: Digital products like e-books or templates can be created once and sold repeatedly. They have high-profit margins and require no physical inventory (Keenan, 2023).

4. Teach Online Courses: Share your knowledge by creating and selling online courses. Although this requires some upfront effort in course creation, you can earn money repeatedly as students enroll (Keenan, 2023).

5. Become a Blogger: If you enjoy sharing your thoughts with others, this is a great way to start making money passively. The good news about this is that it could be through writing or videos; I'm sure you've heard about vlogs. You can monetize your blog through various means, like affiliate marketing and sponsored posts (Keenan, 2023).

6. Start a YouTube channel: This is related to being a blogger or better still, a vlogger. You upload videos based on your interest and your perceived interest in the rest of the world. When you monetize this channel, it can earn you quality money passively. Just so you know, it's a great opportunity to explore because about 2.6 billion people currently use YouTube monthly.

7. Run an Affiliate Marketing Business: Marketing is an evergreen business. It's much more interesting since you can do it and earn money passively. It simply suggests that you are paid a fee for each purchase made through your referral link when you promote a good or service to your audience. It's a straightforward way to add passive income streams (Keenan, 2023).

8. Become a Social Media Influence: This is actually easier than many people think it is. The key is to identify your areas of interest and use them to influence others who could be drawn to similar things via your social media channels. Truly, it's quite easy. Assume you are a fervent comic book lover. You can start posting regularly about the latest news in the comic world, especially from well-known companies like Marvel and DC show. Gradually, people who love comics as much as you do will follow you, and progressively, you'll build an audience. You can then monetize these social media accounts to generate passive income.

9. Rent Out Your Car: If you're not using your car all the time, you can rent it out through services like Turo. Your car can make money for you while you're not actively using it (Keenan, 2023).

10. Open a High-Yield Savings Account: A high-yield savings account offers higher interest rates than traditional savings accounts, allowing your savings to grow passively over time (Keenan, 2023).

These online passive income opportunities provide a fantastic way to kickstart your investment journey. By generating capital through these avenues, you'll have more resources to explore traditional investments like stocks and real estate or even start your own business someday. Another beautiful thing to note is that you can always combine more than one passive income stream. You might, for instance, start and monetize a YouTube channel, grow its social media following, and then include affiliate marketing into it.

Remember, the key is to start early, stay consistent, and keep learning about the world of finance. Good luck on your investment journey, and may your wealth grow steadily over time!

Creating and Selling Digital Products: Tapping into the E-commerce Market

Online sales and distribution of digital goods are possible since they are intangible assets. Electronic books, online classes, music, and other materials are among them. Here's why they matter:

Low Overhead Costs: Unlike physical products, you don't need to worry about storing inventory or shipping costs. This means more money stays in your pocket.

High-Profit Margins: With digital products, there are no ongoing production costs, which means you keep most of what you earn as profit.

Automation: Once you create a digital product, you can sell it repeatedly without much effort. This is passive income, and it's the secret sauce for building wealth over time.

Infinite Possibilities: You can get creative with digital products. Whether you're into art, music, writing, or coding, there's a digital product for you.

Now that you understand the potential let's explore what kinds of digital products you can create and sell:

Educational Products: Are you good at something, like playing an instrument or mastering a video game? You can create online courses or tutorials to teach others.

Licenses for Digital Assets: If you're a budding photographer, musician, or graphic designer, you can sell licenses for your digital creations, like photos, music tracks, or design templates.

Membership Sites: Consider building a website where people pay to access exclusive content. This can be a steady income stream as long as you keep creating valuable content.

Digital Templates and Tools: If you are technologically proficient, you may design digital tools that assist users in issue-solving. Examples include visual design materials, smartphone apps, and résumé templates.

Art Sales: Artists and musicians may sell digital versions of their works of art. It's a lovely way to transform your enthusiasm into money.

Services: If you have skills like web development, digital marketing, or content creation, you can offer your services as digital products.

Here are the steps to kickstart your journey into the world of digital product creation and sales:

Brainstorm Ideas: Think about what you're good at and passionate about. How can you turn that into a digital product? Remember, there are no bad ideas at this stage.

Research Your Niche: Look for online communities, forums, and social media groups related to your chosen niche. What are people talking about? What problems can you help them solve?

Validation: Before diving in, validate your idea. Are people willing to pay for what you're offering? You can do keyword research, check Google Trends, or even ask your potential audience directly.

Create an online store: You'll need an internet platform to sell your digital goods. For those just starting out, Shopify is a user-friendly choice.

You may use a variety of tools and apps to streamline the process. Here are some you might find helpful:

Digital Downloads: A free Shopify app that makes selling digital products on your website easy. Customers can download their purchases instantly.

SendOwl: Ideal for more complex digital product businesses, it offers features like expiring download links and auto-generated license keys.

Courses: If you're selling educational content, this Shopify app allows you to create and sell online courses with ease.

Single Music: Designed for musicians, it bridges the gap between physical and digital music sales.

Thinkific: Perfect for creating and selling online courses, allowing you to upload and organize your course content.

FetchApp: Another option for digital product delivery, offering a free plan for smaller businesses.

Sky Pilot or Bold Memberships: Useful if you plan to build a membership program where customers can access exclusive digital content.

BookThatApp, Tipo, or Sesami: These are great for businesses that offer appointments or consultations as part of their services.

Creating a great product is only the first step. You need to market it effectively:

Lead Magnets: Offer a free, scaled-down version of your product to build an email list and gain trust with potential customers.

Affiliate Programs: Partner with influencers who can promote your product in exchange for a commission on sales.

Collect Preorders: Generate early sales by offering discounts to the first buyers. This can create buzz and generate initial income.

Money-Back Guarantee: Don't be afraid to offer a money-back guarantee. It builds trust and shows you believe in your product.

So, young investor, there you have it. It may be thrilling and rewarding to launch your path to financial independence by producing and selling digital items. It's important to keep in mind that the sooner you begin, the more you can benefit from the amazing power of compound interest.

Workbook 5

1. Have you considered investing in dividend stocks to start building your passive income? Take some time to research and choose a few promising dividend-paying companies.

2. What online opportunities align with your interests and skills? Start exploring how you can leverage the internet to create passive income streams.

3. Have you set specific financial goals for your passive income journey? Define your objectives and create a plan to achieve them.

4. When will you take your first step toward building passive income? Establish a timeline and commit to taking action sooner rather than later.

Takeaway 5

In Chapter 5, we dove into the world of passive income, which is like money that keeps coming in without you actively working for it. It's pretty much like a money-making machine!

First off, we talked about dividend stocks. These are like special stocks that pay you a portion of their earnings regularly. Next up, we looked at rental properties. Where you rent out your property to people who pay you to live on your property or do business there. That's what rental properties are all about. Though it's a great way to generate passive income, you must also ensure not to neglect the responsibilities that come with it, like maintenance.

Lastly, we explored online opportunities. This is like making money through the internet, which is something you probably already do, like selling digital products, offering online courses, or becoming an affiliate for products you love.

So, remember, passive income is like setting up money streams that flow to you, even while you sleep. It's all about making your money work for you!

Chapter 6

Alternative Investment Opportunities

"Diversification is the only free lunch in investing.
-Harry Markowitz

Meet Youssof Altoukhi, a regular 16-year-old who's far from ordinary. He's not your typical teenager – he doesn't just spend his days in school; he's jetting off to conferences in Los Angeles, Dubai, and Geneva. What sets Youssof apart? He's a cryptocurrency entrepreneur who's made a fortune from digital assets. But here's the kicker: he's not alone. There's a new generation of young investors, just like you, who are diving into the world of cryptocurrency and alternative investments.

Imagine making seven figures from cryptocurrency investments like Youssof or selling NFTs like Benyamin Ahmed, who earned £110,000 at just 12 years old. Understanding the financial and technological future is important, rather than merely focusing on getting rich soon. Even if your income isn't in the millions, you may still start planning for your financial future. In this chapter, we'll explore exciting investment avenues beyond traditional stocks, from bonds to cryptocurrencies and more.

Exploring Bonds and Fixed Income Investments

Bonds offer stability and security in the volatile world of finance, where the stock market may resemble a rollercoaster. Bonds are like the steady anchors in the sea of investments. Let me walk you through the world of bonds and fixed-income investments and how they can be your rock when building wealth.

So, what are bonds, exactly? Well, think of them as IOUs. When you buy a bond, you're lending your money to a government or a corporation, and in return, they promise to pay you back with some extra money (interest) at a specific time in the future. Unlike stocks, which represent ownership in a company, bonds are more like a loan you've given to someone else.

Now, let's delve into some science here. Did you know that the concept of bonds isn't limited to finance? In chemistry, a bond is when atoms stick together because they share electrons. It's all about forming a connection. It is actually similar to that. When you buy bonds, you establish a financial relationship with an organization that obligates them to repay you.

Imagine you're on a stormy sea. The waves are wild, and your boat is rocking. In this analogy, the boat is your investment portfolio, and the stormy sea represents the unpredictable stock market. In this situation, you need an anchor to keep you steady. That's where bonds come in.

Here's a scientific fact for you: bonds have a low correlation with stocks. In plain English, this means when stocks go crazy, bonds tend to stay calm. It's like having a backup plan that helps balance out the risks in your investment portfolio. In fact, during turbulent economic times, many investors rush to bonds because they're seen as a safe place to park their money. Bonds provide stability and security when the world seems chaotic.

Let's talk about the perks of having bonds in your financial toolbox. Bonds can provide you with a steady stream of income. Picture this: you invest in a bond, and like clockwork, you receive interest payments. It's almost like having a money tree that reliably produces cash.

Here's another scientific tidbit: bonds can help preserve your capital. Bonds are frequently there to soften the impact when the stock market takes a dip. Your hard-earned money is shielded from being lost by them, acting as a sort of safety net.

Let's skip ahead a little bit now. You are considering your financial future in addition to the immediate profits. Bonds might be crucial in this situation. Adding bonds to your investment portfolio not only lowers your risk it also sets you up for success in the long run.

When you incorporate them into your investing plan, you're not only lowering risk but also setting yourself up for success in the long term.

Remember, bonds offer stability, and in the world of finance, stability is like gold. It's the type of slow growth that might eventually assist you in achieving your financial objectives. Bonds are one of those essential tools. When combined with other investments like stocks, they create a balanced portfolio.

Now, you might wonder why this matters. Well, it's about spreading the risk. Different types of investments perform differently at various times. Having a mix of assets makes you less vulnerable to the ups and downs of a single investment type.

So, my young investor, as you venture into the exciting world of finance, bonds are your steady companions. They provide stability, income, and protection against market turbulence. While they might not offer the thrill of high-flying stocks, bonds are the foundation upon which you can build your financial future.

Bonds occupy a vital spot, ensuring your financial stability today and tomorrow. So, embrace the world of bonds and watch how it redefines your path to financial success. It's a journey worth taking.

Understanding Mutual Funds and ETFs

Alright, young investor, let's dive into the fascinating world of Mutual Funds and ETFs – two vehicles that can help you grow your money. Think of them as your financial building blocks.

Let's talk about Mutual Funds. It could involve you and your friends pooling your money to buy various snacks for a party. Each of you contributes a bit, and together, you have a fantastic spread. That's kind of how mutual funds work. They're a collection of investments, like stocks, bonds, and more, bundled into one big group managed by a professional fund manager.

Now, here's the science bit: mutual funds can be either 'open-ended' or 'closed-end.' Open-ended funds are like a limitless well of shares, creating more shares as more people join in. Conversely, closed-end funds have a fixed number of shares, and you trade them like stocks.

Mutual funds are your go-to if you're into teamwork. They're great for diversifying your investments, meaning you spread your money across many different things. This lowers your risk because if one investment doesn't do well, the others might.

ETFs, or Exchange-Traded Funds, are like the cool solo performers in the investment world. They, too, are a mix of investments, but they act more like individual stocks. You can buy and sell them throughout the trading day, just like you would with your favorite game cards.

ETFs are more flexible when it comes to investment amounts. You can start with as little as the cost of one share, which makes them super accessible for beginners like you. And guess what? They usually have lower fees than mutual funds because they're less 'hands-on' managed.

Here's the scientific twist: ETFs are known for their tax-friendliness. They tend to create fewer tax headaches because they're usually not selling and buying as much as mutual funds. Fewer trades mean fewer taxes to worry about. See, finance and science have a lot in common!

Now, let's say you're in the mutual fund game. You'll usually need more money to get started than ETFs. Some mutual funds require a minimum investment, like $3,000 or $250. These funds have fund managers who work behind the scenes, buying and selling stuff within the fund, aiming to make you a profit. This extra effort comes with slightly higher fees, but that's the cost of having a financial pro on your team.

Mutual funds play by a different set of rules, too. You can only buy or sell them once a day, and the price is set at the end of that trading day, based on something called the 'net asset value' (NAV). Think of it as the total value of everything inside the fund divided by the number of shares.

If you're leaning towards ETFs, you're in for some advantages. ETFs are a breeze to start with because you can buy just one share. No need for a huge pile of cash. Plus, they usually have lower fees, meaning more money stays in your pocket.

The fascinating science part of ETFs is how they're created and redeemed. Large institutional investors do this by assembling all the investments that the ETF tracks and trading them with the ETF provider. This process helps keep the ETF's price close to the actual value of its assets.

ETFs are like the quick-change artists of the investment world. You can buy and sell them anytime during the trading day. No need to wait for the closing bell-like with mutual funds.

The best part is that you are not required to pick a team and remain with it indefinitely. ETFs and mutual funds can both be included in your portfolio. You may get the best of both worlds by combining mutual funds' teamwork and variety with the flexibility and cost-effectiveness of ETFs.

But remember that each player has unique advantages. Mutual funds are like the steady defenders, while ETFs are the agile forwards. Having a mix of both can make your investment game strong.

And one last thing, make sure you always do your research. Look at the fees, check out the past performance, and see which investments are inside the fund or ETF. Understanding what you're investing in is your superpower in the financial world.

So there you have it, the world of Mutual Funds and ETFs unveiled. You've got the teamwork of mutual funds and the flexibility of ETFs. These are your tools for building wealth and securing your financial future.

Precious Metals and Commodities as Investment Assets

Hey there, young investor! Have you ever thought about those shiny treasures known as precious metals and how they can be a part of your investment journey? Well, you're in for a golden lesson. Let's delve into the fascinating world of precious metals like gold, silver, platinum, and the lesser-known palladium.

So, why should you even consider investing in precious metals? These shiny assets offer something truly unique:

Think of precious metals as your financial superheroes, guarding your wealth from the evil clutches of inflation. They maintain their value even when paper money loses its superpowers.

Just like a superhero team, a diversified portfolio is powerful. Precious metals add that diversity by dancing to their own tune, often moving in the opposite direction of stocks and bonds. This helps reduce risks in your investment game.

Now, let's meet the stars of this precious metals show:

Gold is like the rockstar of precious metals. It doesn't rust, it's super malleable, and it conducts heat and electricity like a champ. Unlike most assets, gold's value doesn't follow the supply and demand rhythm; it grooves to the beat of sentiment. When people rush to buy, the price soars; when they sell, it dips.

Gold becomes a sought-after asset in times of financial instability when banks face turbulence and political uncertainty looms, as it is viewed as a safe haven for safeguarding wealth. Additionally, it shines brightly during periods of inflation when other investments lose their luster, serving as a reliable store of value. Moreover, in times of conflict, such as war or political chaos, gold is a portable savior, allowing individuals to protect their savings in the face of turmoil.

Unlike gold, silver is a bit of a shapeshifter. It switches between being a store of value and an industrial metal. This versatility makes its price dance more wildly.

Silver's industrial side shines in:

Once prominent, silver's role in photography diminished as digital cameras took center stage. However, it found new significance in emerging markets with the growth of the middle class, where it became a crucial component in electronics, medical equipment, and various industries. Beyond that, silver became indispensable in the realm of batteries, superconductors, and microcircuits, playing a vital role in powering modern technology and innovation.

Platinum is like that rare gem you can't take your eyes off. It's scarcer than gold, making it more expensive. It's a hotshot in the automotive industry, reducing harmful emissions. However, its price is also influenced by political stability in mining countries and the ebb and flow of auto sales.

Palladium might not be a household name, but it's an unsung hero in the electronics, dentistry, and groundwater treatment industries. It's super shiny and durable, with unique properties making it essential for some industrial applications.

Now, you might be thinking, "How can I invest in these precious metals?" Well, young investor, you've got options:

When it comes to investing in precious metals, you've got a variety of options to choose from. Exchange-traded funds (ETFs) are akin to owning shares in a treasure chest filled with precious metals; they offer easy buying and selling, but you won't have the actual gold bar or silver coin in your possession. Investing in stocks and mutual funds related to precious metals is like embarking on a mining adventure; it's somewhat akin to riding the stock market's rollercoaster, so it's wise to opt for well-managed funds. Futures and options, on the other hand, are the daredevils of the investment world, promising high-profit potential but carrying more risk – think of it as skydiving for your money. If you prefer having the real deal, physical bullion is like having a secret stash of treasure; you own the actual gold or silver, but you'll need a secure place to store it. Lastly, certificates are comparable to magical scrolls pledging you a share of the treasure, but in a genuine crisis, they might end up being nothing more than pieces of paper.

Precious metals aren't your typical investments. They offer protection against inflation, diversification, and a unique way to grow your wealth. They don't pay you regular income like stocks, but they're like an insurance policy for your portfolio.

However, remember that, like superheroes, precious metals have their kryptonite. Prices can drop due to supply and demand imbalances, geopolitical issues, and other factors. But during times of trouble, these superheroes often shine even brighter.

Peer-to-Peer Lending

Are you curious about a cool way to make your money work for you? Well, let's talk about something called Peer-to-Peer (P2P) lending. Consider a situation where you have some extra money and want to expand it, but you don't want to use a large bank. You may investigate P2P lending as you learn about investing since that is where it comes into play.

What is P2P lending, then? It's like a digital marketplace where regular people, just like you and me, can lend money to other regular folks who need a loan. It's a bit like being a banker but without the bank! Instead of dealing with a traditional financial institution, you connect directly with people who need money through special websites.

These websites, like Prosper, Lending Club, Upstart, and Funding Circle, act as matchmakers. They help borrowers find lenders and vice versa. It resembles a virtual handshake between individuals looking to lend money and those looking to borrow it.

This is how it goes: You establish an account as a lender on one of these P2P lending websites and add funds to it. Loans will be financed using this money. On the other hand, those needing loans set up profiles outlining their needs and repayment strategies. Based on their financial situation, they're assigned an interest rate.

Now, as a lender, you can look at these profiles and decide who you want to lend your money to. You might choose to lend a little to several people or a larger amount to just one. It's like being in control of your own mini-bank.

The cool thing is that you can often earn more interest on the money you lend through P2P lending compared to a regular savings account or a certificate of deposit (CD). But, and it's a big but, there's a catch – just like in real banking, there's a risk that the people who borrow your money might not pay it back.

That's where P2P lending gets interesting and a bit tricky. As a lender, you take on more risk than traditional banks. Research shows that more than 10% of borrowers occasionally default on their obligations. This is far more than what banks usually deal with.

But hey, P2P lending can be an intriguing approach to start investing if you're prepared to take a little risk and want to perhaps boost your return on investment. And it's also a way to help others.

You might now be asking how commonplace peer-to-peer lending is. So, it's expanding. The global P2P lending market was worth around $134.35

billion in 2022, and it's expected to reach a whopping $705.81 billion by 2030. That's a pretty huge playground for investors and borrowers alike!

There you have it—a succinct overview of the P2P lending industry. As you gain more knowledge about budgeting and increasing your funds, you may study what it's like to be a banker in the modern era. You'll be on your way to being a wise adolescent investor if you just keep the hazards in mind and do your study.

Investing in Cryptocurrencies: Risks and Rewards

You've probably heard a lot of chatter about cryptocurrencies like Bitcoin. They're akin to digital cash that folks use to make purchases or invest, and they've been grabbing headlines. However, similar to any other investment, there are vital aspects to grasp regarding the pros and cons of wading into cryptocurrencies.

Let's kick things off by discussing the rewards. Cryptocurrencies have been minting some individuals a heap of cash. Picture buying something for a few bucks and later selling it for thousands! That's precisely what's been going down with Bitcoin and some other cryptocurrencies. It's like striking digital gold.

Here's another nifty bit – certain businesses are starting to embrace cryptocurrencies as a legit mode of payment. So, you might be able to use your crypto coins to snag things you fancy, just like good ol' regular money. It's quite thrilling because it underscores the increasing significance of cryptocurrencies in our world.

Now, let's delve into the risks; believe me, there are a bunch. First and foremost, cryptocurrencies aren't akin to the dough you've got stashed in your wallet. They aren't backed by any government, which means there's no safety net if things take a nosedive. If you happen to misplace your crypto or get hoodwinked, there's no cavalry to ride to your rescue. It's like the Wild West out here.

The world of cryptocurrencies is full of frauds, speaking of which, people are being duped into handing up their digital currency, and once those coins vanish into thin air, they're gone forever. Scammers are absolutely smitten with cryptocurrencies because they can be a tough nut to crack, making it darn hard to collar 'em.

To add some extra spice, cryptocurrency prices can be utterly bonkers. They can reach the upper atmosphere one day and the lowest levels the next. It's like getting on a rollercoaster, and not everyone is built to experience that kind of exhilaration. Your investment can skyrocket while also having a substantial possibility of plummeting.

Let me share this pearl of wisdom: Cryptocurrencies are created on a technology known as blockchain. It's like a super-secure digital ledger that logs every crypto transaction. Yet, even with all this technological wizardry, there are still pitfalls. Bad actors can break into crypto exchanges and make off with the loot, and that's the last thing you want to happen.

Here's one more angle to ponder – some banks and businesses are also dipping their toes into the cryptocurrency pool. Sounds nifty, right? But it also implies they're rolling the dice. If things go south in crypto, it could send ripples across the entire financial landscape, and that's no small potatoes.

So, what's the big takeaway? Cryptocurrencies can be an exhilarating path to potentially rake in the green and use it to snag cool stuff, but they come with hefty caveats. It's akin to riding a slick new bike without training wheels – you can have a blast, but you've got to tread cautiously.

Remember: if you decide to wade into the cryptocurrency waters, do your homework. Gobble up knowledge like it's your favorite snack, and don't throw in money you can't afford to part with. It's akin to picking up a new game or sport – you want to grasp the rules before you dive in. And if you ever find yourself in doubt or with burning questions, it's wise to have a chinwag with someone you trust, like your folks or a financial whiz.

Venture Capital and Startups

You know, the world of startups can be like an exciting adventure. Let's say you're a member of a team that has a brilliant concept that has the potential to transform society or open up a brand-new market. But much like any journey, it needs resources to be accomplished. I'm here to give you the dirt on venture capital, which is where it comes into play.

Venture Capital - The Cool and the Not So Cool:

Let's start with the cool stuff. Imagine having a brilliant idea and getting a pile of cash to turn it into reality. That's what venture capital (VC) is all about. When startups get VC support, they suddenly have access to a treasure chest of money. This cash injection can help them hire smart people, build amazing products, and market them to the world. It's like turbocharging your startup.

But wait, there's more! Venture capitalists aren't just moneybags. They're like Yoda from Star Wars but for startups. They bring wisdom and experience to the table. These folks have seen it all in the business world and are ready to share their secrets with you. Think of them as your startup's mentors, helping you dodge obstacles and make smart decisions.

Now, let's talk about the not-so-cool side of things. When you take VC money, you're not the sole captain of your ship anymore. You have to share control with the venture capitalists. They become like your co-pilots, making big decisions alongside you. So, if you're used to having total control, this can be a bit tricky.

And here's the kicker – when you take that VC cash, you're also giving away slices of your company. Imagine baking a delicious pie and then having to

share it with more people. That's what happens to your ownership. You'll own less of your business, which means you get a smaller slice of the profits.

Another thing to know is that venture capitalists are like the speed police on the highway. They want you to hit the gas pedal hard and go super-fast. They're not in it for a leisurely Sunday drive. They expect you to grow like crazy and make them a lot of money – and fast. It's like having a deadline hanging over your head, which may be stressful.

Here's where science enters the picture: Did you realize that risk is at the heart of venture capital? Yes, it resembles a high-stakes game. Most businesses fail, which is a scientific truth, and venture funders are fully aware of this. They invest in a bunch of startups, hoping that one or two will become massive successes. It's a bit like planting a lot of seeds and hoping some grow into giant oak trees.

Another scientific tidbit – VC can be like a rocket booster for startups. You may recruit the brightest minds, create incredible technology, and expand more quickly than you ever could on your own when you receive that capital infusion. It's a rollercoaster, though, with many ups and downs, much like a rocket launch.

The conclusion is then? Venture capital is like a magic wand for startups but comes with a price. You get money, guidance, and connections but also give up some control and ownership. It's similar to joining a superhero team in that you earn abilities but also have to cooperate with your teammates.

The thing is this: if you're considering taking this route, do your research. Make sure you're ready for the fast lane and that your goals align with your investors. And remember, it's okay to explore other funding options too. Venture financing does not need you to invest everything.

Venture money is akin to a superpower in the startup sector. The world could change if you use it wisely. Recall that enormous power comes with great responsibility. And if you ever feel lost in the startup galaxy, don't hesitate to seek guidance from wise mentors or your parents. You've got this!

Environmental, Social, and Governance (ESG) Investing

ESG stands for Environmental, Social, and Governance. Investors might use these three terms as a kind of checklist to determine whether a firm is performing good deeds for society and running its business well.

Environmental concerns involve checking if a company is treating Mother Earth kindly. This means looking at how much energy they use, the pollution they create, and whether they're fighting climate change. Interestingly, studies suggest that eco-friendly companies can actually rake in more green in the long run (Smith & Chang, 2020).

Social considerations delve into a company's approach to people, including how they treat their workers, treat everyone equally, and act as good neighbors in their neighborhood. The cool part is that companies with a friendly attitude often attract more customers and talented folks (American slang for people).

Lastly, governance is like inspecting how a company is run; it checks if they're playing by the rules, making honest decisions, and having a top-notch leadership team. Companies with strong governance tend to be more solid and less likely to end up in hot water (Bebchuk & Weisbach, 2010). So, it's like making sure a company is kind to the environment and people while being a good rule-follower and leader in the business world

So, why should a teenager like you care about ESG investing?

Placing your money in businesses that are working to improve the world means investing with ESG or environmental, social, and governance issues. As if to say, "I want to use my investments to do some good." And guess what? It's not just a feel-good move; it can also fill up your wallet. Studies hint that companies with high ESG scores might just perform like rock stars in the stock market over time, so you're not just doing good; you're cashing in on it! Plus, you're not just another investor but a message sender. You're telling companies that care for the planet, treat folks right, and have their act together in leadership that their efforts matter. You're basically saying, "Keep up the good work!"

Now, I know what you might be thinking: "How can a teenager like me start ESG investing?" It's a great question! While you might not have much money to invest right now, you can start learning about it. Ask your parents or guardians if they can help you open a practice investment account. You can then use fake money to practice making ESG investments and see how it all works. It's like a game where you learn to be a responsible investor.

Social considerations delve into a company's approach to people, including how they treat their workers, treat everyone equally, and act as good neighbors in their neighborhood.

So, ESG investing isn't just for adults—it's something you can start exploring now, and who knows, you might become a savvy ESG investor in the future!

The world is changing, and many people believe that investing in companies that do good is the way forward. By understanding ESG, you're getting a head start on a future where responsible investing is not just a choice but a smart one.

Keep learning, keep exploring, and you'll do great things!

Sustainable and Impact Investing

You know, the money game isn't just for the grown-ups. Teens like you can dive right in, and here's the cool part – you can invest with a mission. Believe it or not, you can use your moolah to back companies that are all about boosting our world.

So, what's this cool kid lingo for it? It's called sustainable and impact investing. But before we dive in, let's break it down so it's as clear as day.

Sustainable and impact investing means putting your money into companies that aren't just about making profits. They're also working hard to do good things for the planet and its people. It's like saying, "I want to help make the world a better place with my investments."

Now, you might be thinking, "Okay, that sounds sweet, but does it actually make money?" Well, here's the cool part – studies suggest that companies with high scores in sustainable and impact investing can perform even better in the stock market over time. So, while you're doing good, you might also make some money!

But it's not just about the cash. By supporting these awesome companies, you're sending a message. You're telling businesses that being responsible and caring about things like the environment, treating their employees right, and having good leadership are important to you. And when companies see that, they keep doing good things.

You see, it's all about making your money work for you and the world. So, how can you get started with this super cool investing? Well, it's like a simple ABC framework:

A - Avoid: This is like saying, "I don't want my money going to companies that harm the environment or treat people poorly." So, you can choose to avoid investing in those companies.

B - Benefit: Here, you're saying, "I want to support companies that are doing good things." It's like putting your money into businesses that care about the environment or have cool social practices.

C - Contribute: This is the big one. You're expressing the desire to "invest in businesses with a real, measurable impact." These are the people making a conscious effort to improve the world by decreasing carbon emissions.

And guess what? It's not just for grown-ups. Teens like you can totally get in on this action. You can start small and learn the ropes. There are resources and advisors out there who can help you figure it all out.

Keep in mind it's not solely about raking in the bucks; it's about putting your money where your heart is – in a world that's getting better every day. We're all part of this journey; even the smallest contributions make a big difference. As the saying goes, "You can be the driving force for the change you want in the world." So, why not put your cash behind that change too?

Investing in Emerging Technologies

Emerging technologies are like those super cool gizmos you can't wait to get your hands on – but they're not just for kicks. They're reshaping the world, and guess what? You can be part of the action. Let's break it down.

To start, what exactly are these emerging technologies we're jazzed about? Think of them as the superheroes of the tech realm, poised to revolutionize our lives in the next decade. One heavyweight in this league is Artificial Intelligence (AI). AI is primed to become a trillion-dollar industry by 2030, with a faster growth rate than a speeding bullet (well, almost!). It's all thanks to the demand for image processing, identification technology, and yes, big data.

Then, there's Robotics. Robots are taking charge in various sectors like healthcare, agriculture, and manufacturing. By 2030, the robotics market could be worth a jaw-dropping $149.86 billion! Why, you ask? Because we're all about automation and safety, and these mechanical marvels are here to deliver.

Lastly, let's talk Mobile Technology. That covers everything from your trusty smartphone to tablets and laptops – tech that's with you wherever you roam. The mobile app market alone is poised to hit $565.4 billion by

2030! Can you believe it? So, you can bet there's a treasure trove of opportunities in the mobile tech world.

Now, you might be thinking, "How can I get in on these awesome technologies?" Well, there are a couple of ways to do it.

Stocks – If you're itching to dive headfirst into the tech scene, stocks are your golden ticket. You can grab shares of companies deep into AI, robotics, or mobile tech. It's like owning a slice of the pie. Take a gander at lists of companies in these fields to kick things off.

ETFs – If you're aiming to spread your bets across a bunch of companies all at once, Exchange-Traded Funds (ETFs) are your go-to. They're like a smorgasbord of tech treasures, and they help play it safe. Look into ETFs zoned in on AI, robotics, or tech as a whole.

Now, here comes the fun part – why should this matter to you? Aside from being incredibly thrilling, investing in emerging technologies can be a game-changer. You may also receive some scrumptious returns on your investments and the opportunity to participate in the newest and best developments.

It's crucial to remember that gaining money isn't everything; investing in a better world is. We are all in this together; therefore, every single effort counts. Why not contribute to that change as well? After all, "Be the change you wish to see in the world."

So, whether you're daydreaming about AI, robotics, or the next mega-hit mobile app, know this – you can be a savvy tech investor, even as a teenager. The future is yours to mold, one investment at a time. Get out there, explore, and let your investments be the heroes of your financial journey!

Investment Strategies that Work

Investment strategies may sound like a term meant for grown-ups in suits, but guess what? Even as a teenager, you can dive into this exciting world and start building your financial future. Let me break it down for you.

First things first, what are investment strategies? Think of them as game plans for your money. They help you decide where and how to invest based on how much you want to earn, how much risk you can handle, and how long you plan to invest. These strategies are like your GPS, guiding your money toward your goals.

Now, let's talk about some of these strategies you can consider:

Imagine you're investing in the stock market. Passive strategy is like buying some stocks and holding onto them for a while, hoping they'll grow over time. It's a bit like planting seeds and waiting for them to become big, beautiful trees. On the other hand, active strategy is more like gardening. You buy and sell stocks frequently, trying to make quick gains. It's riskier because you're constantly making moves.

Growth Investing is like betting on a horse you believe will win the race. If you think a company will grow a lot in the future, you invest in it for the long term. But if you expect a quicker win, you might go for short-term investments, like saving up for a big purchase.

Ever heard of Warren Buffett? He's famous for this strategy. It's like going to a garage sale and finding a hidden treasure. You look for stocks undervalued in the market, hoping their prices will go up when the market realizes its mistake. That's what is called Value Investing.

Income Investing is like having a money tree that keeps giving you cash. Instead of relying on stock prices going up, you invest in stocks that pay regular dividends or in bonds that give you interest payments. It's a steady income source.

Dividend Growth Investing means you invest in companies that pay dividends and increase them year after year. It's like getting a raise at your part-time job but with stocks. Over time, those small raises can turn into big money.

Imagine everyone's selling their video game consoles because they think video games are no longer cool. As a contrarian investor, you swoop in and buy those consoles at a discount. When video games become cool again, you sell them for a nice profit.

Think of indexing as buying a little bit of everything. Instead of picking individual stocks, you invest in a piece of the entire stock market, like the S&P 500. It's like having a slice of every pizza at a pizza party.

Now, why should you even care about investment strategies? Well, it's not just about making money (although that's a nice perk). It's about making your money work for you. Choosing the right strategy allows you to grow your savings over time and be better prepared for big goals like college or buying a car.

Here's the scoop: The sooner you start, the more time your money has to grow. Let's say you invest $100 today, and it grows by 7% every year. In 10 years, you'll have around $196. But if you wait another 10 years to invest that $100, you'll end up with only about $386. Starting early is like giving your money a head start in a race.

Keep in mind that every investment has some amount of risk. Like learning to ride a bike, you may make mistakes at first, but you improve with time and practice. Setting objectives, doing research, and perhaps even seeking out professional guidance are crucial for this reason.

So, don't wait too long to start your investment journey. Even a small amount can grow into something significant over time. Your financial future is like a puzzle, and these strategies are your puzzle pieces. Start putting them together, and you'll see the bigger picture of financial success.

Workbook 6

1. Imagine you have $1,000 to invest and are interested in exploring diverse investment avenues. Based on what you've learned, which investment options would you consider and why? Create a simple investment plan outlining where you'd allocate your money.

2. You're passionate about environmental issues and want your investments to reflect that. How would you incorporate ESG (Environmental, Social, and Governance) investing principles into your portfolio? What steps would you take to ensure your investments align with your values?

3. Research one emerging investment opportunity that intrigues you the most, like renewable energy, AI, or biotechnology. Write a short report explaining why this field interests you and how you can start investing in it.

4. You've saved $500, and you want to try your hand at investing. Describe your investment goals and risk tolerance. Then, choose one investment avenue from the list and explain how it matches your objectives.

5. Cryptocurrencies have been making headlines lately. Do some research on cryptocurrencies, their potential risks, and rewards. Based on your findings, would you consider investing a small portion of your savings in cryptocurrencies? Why or why not?

6. Imagine you have a friend who's hesitant about investing. After learning about diverse investment avenues, how would you explain the benefits of investing simply and convincingly to encourage your friend to take action and start investing?

Takeaway 6

Alright, let's sum up the important stuff from our investment journey. You've learned that investing isn't just for adults in suits – even as a teenager, you can get in on the action. We talked about various strategies, like passive and active investing, growth, value, income, dividend growth, contrarian, and indexing. Each strategy is like a tool in your financial toolbox, helping you reach your goals.

We also explored diverse investment avenues like bonds, mutual funds, precious metals, cryptocurrencies, ESG (which is all about investing for a better planet), peer-to-peer lending, and emerging investments. These are like different paths you can take on your investment adventure. Some might be smooth rides, while others have a few bumps along the way. Either way, ensure to keep learning, stay curious, and watch your money grow!

Part 3

Empowering Your Financial Future

Chapter 7

Investing in Yourself, Education, and Skills

"All our dreams can come true if we have the courage to pursue them."
— **Walt Disney**

Shifting from a Short-Term to a Long-Term Financial Mindset

A short-term financial mindset is a mindset that focuses on what to do now to make money. This mindset doesn't consider the future or what will happen when the money is exhausted. A short-term financial mindset aims to get something and use it now, and when it's gone, get another one.

It's like a circle of poverty that never ends. People with this mindset make money to feed or sort bills, pay fees, or rent. Once the pressing needs in their lives are met, they are satisfied and wait till another need arises.

These kinds of people never rise above their means. They live dependent on a particular source and learn to "cut their coats according to their size" all their lives. The real challenge in this type of living is that if they lose that one source of livelihood they depend on, their frustration and poverty know no bounds. They get stuck in life.

As a teen, you might find that you're prone to this mindset because you may feel you're still very young and have a lot of years ahead of you. Aside from the years you have ahead, you may believe your parents or guardians have your future covered or that somehow, when you get to that bridge, you'll cross it.

Other reasons for this mindset may be your family background or the limited and poor mindset a person might have had about money while growing up. Maybe all you saw was your parents working two or three jobs just to make ends meet. You may grow up thinking that's how life is meant to be.

This mentality can lead to reckless and irresponsible spending, lack, and, in the nearest future, poverty. Having a short-term financial mindset won't do you much good. You need to shift your mindset to a long-term financial mindset if you hope to make anything reasonable out of your future.

A long-term financial mindset has your future at the center of its plans. This mindset enables you to establish financial wallets that can last into your tomorrow and not just end in satisfying your today.

This kind of mindset requires rational thinking and planning. This mindset educates you on investing in other things more valuable than money, like relationships, loyalty, networks, etc. It teaches discipline and strategic planning.

To understand the difference between short-term and long-term financial mindset, imagine a marketer who would rather sell his goods to 200 average Joes than 3 wealthy people (yes, I know he has to be crazy, but that's the point).

He fails to realize that while the average Joes can give him a good amount of money, it can't be compared to the money, connections, and referrals that 3 wealthy people can bring.

This marketer is looking at the now and not at the future. He forgets that a few wealthy people who purchase his product can lead him to more wealthy people via referrals. That way, his business is growing financially and in its reputation. When people see the wealthy people that troop to his business, other wealthy people will come hoping to find quality.

Nevertheless, it's important to strike a balance between both financial mindsets. A long-term financial mindset on its own is not good enough, just as having a short-term financial mindset isn't good if that's the entirety of your financial approach. That's because if you only plan on how to settle the now, the latter will be left undone. On the other hand, if you focus only on the future and ignore the now, you may not live to enjoy that future you're planning for.

Living in the present and planning for the future are equally important. You need to have a financial plan that enables you to feed the needs of the now and still have enough to save for the future, not just the rainy days. I know, you may say, I don't get paid enough.

Well, no amount is too small to save, and the law of savings applies to everyone. If you save a dollar today and another tomorrow, you'll have two dollars, not one. This law works for the rich and the poor.

So, how do you spend and save the little or plenty you earn? The method is simple:

- Draft a list of what you want in order of priority. When you draft this list, divide them into categories.

- Divide your earnings in percentages to the categories in order of importance.

- Once you've decided on the percentage, convert each percentage to dollars and write it after each category.

- Once you get your earnings, divide them as you've stated.

It's important you make this list before you receive your earnings, and the reason is simple: when you have a list, you're more likely to follow it and do something reasonable with your money. If there's no list, you'll end up spending the money on whatever comes.

Knowing what to do with your earnings guides you in spending. You find out you don't spend more than you should. You will also discover that most of your necessary needs are met, and you still have some left as savings.

Now, as you save that percentage from time to time, you'll discover that you'd have saved enough money to invest in something tangible. Moreso, there's another law of savings: Never Touch Your Savings. Your savings are only meant for producing more money.

As you save, seek investment opportunities around you. It's important you ask the right people and ensure your source is authentic. You don't want to lose your savings on scam investments. You can ask your counselors, parents, or visit a bank and ask for investment options. You can't go wrong with a bank.

Investing is simply using money to get more money. When you've got a reliable source, start investing your savings. As you invest, continue saving. When you've saved another reasonable amount, invest it again in another profitable venture.

If possible, seek ventures that have a future probability. Some ventures are temporary or stagnant. Seek ventures that are always in demand and can never go out of demand. Once your investment starts paying, reinvest the money in a higher aspect of that venture or another venture.

This way, you get to settle your present needs while securing your future. So, as a teen, you can start saving now. If you don't have a job, you can save from the gifts you receive from family and friends. Remember, savings don't have to start with thousands. You can save your hundreds to get to thousands. Start saving today for a better future.

The Power of Lifelong Learning

As the Arabian saying goes,

"He who knows not,

and knows not that he knows not,

is a fool; shun him.

He who knows not,

and knows that he knows not,

is a student; Teach him.

He who knows,

and knows not that he knows,

is asleep; Wake him.

He who knows,

and knows that he knows,

is Wise; Follow him."

Lifelong learning is the pass that gets you into the "Wise" class. Lifelong learning is the conscious investment into learning as a way of life. It goes beyond just learning a new skill now and then.

According to Pew Research, 73% of adults are said to be lifelong learners. It means they pursue knowledge while working and also way after retirement (Horrigan, 2016).

In lifelong learning, you're dedicated to pursuing the path of knowledge and education for as long as you live. So learning doesn't end after bagging a few degrees and professional certificates. Learning doesn't stop after acquiring a few skills or branching out to other fields of study and getting certificates. No. Here, learning is a way of life.

This is important, especially in our current society, because the world keeps evolving. For instance, at the start of technological advancements, we had VCRs, CDs, paper road maps, floppy disk drives, photo labs, etc. In those days, these proved effective and seen as performing wonders in the eyes of the average man. Today, however, some of these technologies have gone obsolete while some others are barely available. What we have today in place of these technologies is almost a hundred times faster, better, and more efficient. That's to show the evolution that is going on in the world. The thing with this evolution is that it is not limited to one aspect of society alone but in every area of society. There is a change in our wedding pattern, method of cooking, mode of communication, etc.

Now, if you choose to learn and stop, you may wake up tomorrow and discover that the world has moved on, leaving you behind. Therefore, it's important that both teens and adults develop a lifelong learning mindset.

The more you learn, the more exposed you become and the wilder your imagination. The wilder your imagination, the broader your scope and ability to even create new things of your own. Learning keeps your mind active, and this improves the cognitive abilities in both adults and teens. For adults, it reduces the probability of having dementia.

People who dedicate their lives to always learning never lose relevance in society. As a teen, you will naturally tower above your age mates, and as an adult, even after retirement, you can serve as a tutor in any area you are strong in.

Moreover, modern-day technology has made lifelong learning a lot easier. Today, you can enroll in classes online. You can learn almost anything online. Some classes are free, and others have a price tag. But the advantage of it is that you can learn remotely.

Aside online classes, physical classes abound everywhere in various fields. You don't need to travel miles to learn a skill or get a certificate. Furthermore, if you don't have the time to attend a class or take a course online, you can read to educate yourself.

You can pick various subjects of life or business you wish to learn about and start researching them one after the other. You can read blogs/ e-books or listen to podcasts.

All of these are ways of gaining or/and improving your knowledge in various areas, and it's all part of lifelong learning. You don't have an excuse why you would stop learning. Remember, if you can't attend classes, read, and if you can't read, listen. Whatever method you choose, just keep learning so you'll flow with the world as it moves on.

Acquiring Marketable Skills

Marketable skills are skills that increase your chances of getting a job. These skills can be a hobby, an area of interest, or a skill required to make you better in your field. These skills are different from your formal education. Here's a short story that can help you understand this better.

John and Jude are both applying for the same job as customer care reps. John's CV is rich but limited to two BSc degrees and a master's degree in Communications.

On the other hand, Jude's CV has one BSc degree and a master's degree in Communications, various certifications in short-term communication courses, and other soft skills.

Between them, Jude is more marketable than John because of his extra skills and is more likely to get the job. You see, it's important to bag degrees, but that shouldn't be the end.

Lots of employers aren't just looking for degree holders alone. They need to know you're capable of applying the knowledge you've acquired, actually doing the job, and even adding to the company's growth. No company needs a liability, like people they'll employ with degrees and have to spend more money training them.

Such persons end up doing what they have been trained to do. They are hard workers and may bring money to the company but may never be a part of the company's creativity that boosts it. As time passes and the company improves, they may remain with the old knowledge of what they've been taught.

Therefore, to convince a company of your capabilities and potential, you need to show them the skills you've acquired that align with the job you're applying for. This way, your marketability increases because they see an asset that will get right into the job. They see an asset they only need to develop for optimal performance.

Furthermore, when you acquire marketable skills that boost your resume, you are more likely to seek to improve when you finally get the job. You will naturally have the motivation to learn, improve, and add more skills in that area. That's what every company desires.

Even as a teen, you can start acquiring some skills. It doesn't have to be anything too professional, like programming or accounting. It can be improving on a hobby or area of interest, like painting, writing, or learning a craft.

As you grow older, and have a clearer picture of who you hope to become, you can start delving into useful skills that boost your resume and increase your marketability.

To know what skills you need to acquire, you must first examine where you want to get to. Picture the kind of job you want to do and the height you hope to reach in that field. Secondly, outline the skills you have now and how they relate to your job (s) of interest.

Next, make a list of skills that are paramount and will distinguish you in your job (s) of interest. Once you've made this list, start a new list. Write down the skills you already have that make you markable in that area, and start learning other necessary skills you don't have yet.

Once you acquire a new skill, add it to the list of your skills. The more you do this, the more marketable you will become. You can use your teen

125

days to acquire these skills. Some of these skills can be acquired in months or even a year. That means in two to three years, you must have acquired five to seven skills to boost your resume.

As you go on to acquire skills, try as much as possible to acquire skills with certifications. Certifications are like proofs the company can hold onto.

Two types of skills are necessary for your marketability:

- Hard skills: These are acquired physical skills that boost your resume and make you employable. They are also known as employability skills.

- Soft skills: These are certain values, traits, and principles acquired that boost your leadership qualities and overall personality. They're also known as transferable skills.

Both types of skills are important for a person to acquire. Some hard skills include:

- Copywriting

- Graphics design

- Programming language

- Search Engine Optimization (SEO)

- Financial analysis

- Coding

- Marketing

- Photography

- Typing

- Photo editing

- Foreign language

- Plumbing

- Cinematography

- Acting

- Video editing

- Social media marketing

- Sales

- Structured Query Language (SQL)

There are lots of them. You don't have to do all of them, though. If you already have a job, select hard skills to help you improve. However, your improvement shouldn't be temporary. Seek skills that will remain relevant in that field's future growth and development.

Aside from hard skills, there are soft skills. Here are some examples of soft skills:

- Critical thinking

- Integrity

- Adaptability

- Conflict resolution

- Creativity

- Professionalism

- Good communication skills

- Interpersonal skills

- Active listening

- Confidence

- Trustworthy

- Industrious

- Patience

- Management

- Problem-solving

- Tolerance

These skills are different from hard skills because they are not tangible but are quite important. No employer wants to condone an intelligent but rude and rascally employee.

For instance, imagine you walk into an organization to enquire about their business only to be encountered by a rude and lousy receptionist. That attitude from one employee alone, though capable, can tarnish the image of that company, and if that company has two or three of those in important sections, it may not last long.

Therefore, as you acquire certifications, acquire the soft skills needed for that job.

Understanding the Value of Education Investment

According to the World Literacy Foundation, 3 billion people find it difficult to read and write (as cited by Miranda, 2022). It's alarming that as easy as education has become today, illiteracy is still on the rampage.

Some people see education as a waste of money, while others simply do not have the money to invest in it. However, the benefits of education are incontestable. It adds knowledge and value to your life. With education, you can venture into any aspect of the world and create a positive impact.

As a teen, you need to understand that education is important if you hope to become someone to reckon with in life. I know that as a teen, you'd prefer to attend parties, cheat during exams, and spend your time socializing, but it begins to tell on you in the long run.

Imagine meeting a cute young man of 20 years. He speaks fluently, but when asked to read or spell his name, he can't because he isn't educated. That alone will automatically wash off all his physical charms.

As a teen, don't program your mind to procrastinate learning. You may find out it's too late before you realize it. But one good thing about education is that there is no age limit. Yet, it's important to start early.

Investing in education is simply exchanging money for knowledge. This increases literacy, and it adds innumerable benefits to individuals and society at large.

Firstly, literates find it easy to get a good-paying job and be an asset. This way, they can take care of their families and raise more literates who will continue the circle. The more literates we raise in society, the better society becomes.

Furthermore, investing in education improves the economy of the nation. Whether investing as a student or opening an educational institution as a business, it'll improve the economy. Those who open businesses due to their acquired knowledge provide more job opportunities for others.

In addition, education trims off ignorance and makes individuals more responsible. It molds individuals who are sympathetic and caring. These individuals talk reasonably and make reasonable decisions. They are confident and have healthy self-esteem because the knowledge they have makes them feel relevant.

Aside from that, they live healthy and happy lives. That's because they understand the importance of proper feeding and know how to read their body. They know the importance of exercise and medical check-ups. That's because they have learned about it. Knowledge, they say, is power.

Again, education exposes you to things you may never have known outside of it. You're exposed to a new lifestyle, languages, cultures, fields, etc. It also sharpens your potential and gives you the confidence to develop them and the right information to use them correctly.

Education fashions your mind and both deepens and widens your imagination. It pushes you to want to become someone to reckon with in life. It brings you out of mediocrity, and you aspire to be at the top.

It opens your eyes to see a greatness in you that you never even dreamed of before. It develops you and helps you cultivate a positive and mature mindset.

It makes you creative and innovative. When you're educated, you acquire the ability and capacity to think outside the box and carry out your thoughts professionally. You can think of new ways to do things and solve problems, even at home.

In the end, literates give back to society, thereby improving the condition of society. Some of them teach the young ones, while others start up NGOs reaching hundreds and millions of illiterates. This way, a better society is crafted by the hands of the literate.

Education touches and transforms every area of your life – physically, emotionally, mentally and otherwise – therefore, its importance cannot be underestimated. It doesn't just improve the lives of individuals but that of families and society at large.

Balancing Investments in Yourself and Financial Assets

Paul is an average earner with a family of five. He loves to take his family out to nice places. His family is always happy, and the bills are always paid, however, when he retires, he has nothing to fall back to, not even a house of his own.

On the other hand, Jake is an average earner with a family of three. He knows a lot about the benefits of investment and puts in as much as he can into different investments. He doesn't have time or money for outings or such things. He pays his bills, but that's as much as he does. After retirement, he finds he has a lot of money but no one to spend it with because his kids are all grown and are away.

Lastly, we see Corner, also an average earner with a family of five, who plans vacations for his family twice a year. His children are all in school; he pays his bills and has enough to invest in his retirement plan. He still saves up a token from his pay and invests it in securing a house. It's on lease, but he's paying it up.

After retirement, he has enough to start a small business and make other investments.

This is an example of those who focus on financial investment over self-investment and vice versa and those who can strike a balance.

You may be among those who believe that self-investment is very profitable and valuable. You spend your years and earnings acquiring degrees, skills, and certifications, all in the bid to be extra valuable. In the end, you actually achieve your goal but with no reasonable financial assets.

Now, it may not even be that you don't have savings. You may pride yourself in the monthly savings you make. However, in the end, you'll find it isn't enough to cater to all your needs after retirement.

And, indeed, your skills can still fetch you money even when you're old, as long as they're valuable, but then, using the skills you've acquired while growing for money as a retiree isn't the dream. It means you'll keep struggling till it's too late. At this point, you'll then realize how important financial investments are for the future. This is one extreme.

On the other extreme, you may believe in investing so much in financial assets (liquid assets like bonds, shares, stocks, etc) and very little in yourself.

This set of people feel investing in financial assets is more profitable because they actually get returns. These returns motivate them to branch out and invest in as many financial assets as they can afford.

With this belief, you're ready to open an account and start an investment for all your kids. It's the only thing you ever talk about when you're among people. You pay little attention to adding value to your life.

You may prosper in your investments but stagnate or depreciate in other areas, especially your work. That's because you're not adding new and improved knowledge that you can apply to your work. You'll keep doing the same thing you've been doing from the beginning the same way you've been doing it.

At the end of the day, you'll be left with so much money with little or no knowledge of what to do with it. At this time, you may even be too old to learn the skill you would have loved to learn. Or the opportunity to utilize it would have gone.

Perhaps, if you had had that skill, you would have done better and been promoted at work. You could probably have had other important things to teach your grandkids at this time, or you'd have been the one the family would come to for help when they needed to understand programming or coding.

However, because you didn't learn anything with all the money you have, you have nothing but money now to give.

Both parties are the extremists of both investments, which is wrong. There's a need to establish a balance between both self and financial investment. They're both equally important with peculiar benefits. So, in life, you need to learn to balance them.

You can make a short-term financial investment to pay for and learn a course in graphics design, coding, or content writing. You can then make long-term financial investments for your retirement or to own a home. This is how to use your financial investment in investing in yourself.

This way, you don't get to miss out on both worlds. You can have their benefits in full. So at the end of the day, you have value to dish out and money to prove it.

Know that both ideas can only succeed when there is a balance because one empowers you to be relevant, while the other makes a happy future.

Investing in a Globalized World

Technology has made the world we live in today a global village. People and places can be reached at your fingertips. Today, you can purchase something online, shipped from another country, and delivered to your doorstep. You can even order a pizza or Chinese via an app, and it'll be delivered in little time. Everything is easy.

Also, these days, many services are offered by online providers. This means you don't need to sell goods before you can get money. You can offer services like tutoring, counseling, marketing, etc, all online.

Due to the globalization of the world, the business world has expanded and broken boundaries. Many limitations have been managed, like moving cash in vans from one place to another to purchase goods. Today, you don't even need to visit a bank to make a transfer. You only need the right codes and apps on your smartphone.

All of these have created avenues for both small and large investments. It means both teens and adults can find a place to invest what they have. As a teenager who is up to 18 or 21, if you have some savings, you can open a brokerage account where you can invest in bonds, stocks, ETFs, and mutual funds.

On the other hand, parents/guardians can open a custodial account for minors. This account serves as a savings account for their kids' future. The account is opened in the child's name, but the legal right of control is solely on the parents/guardians until the child comes of age.

Teens can also invest in a ROTH account once they start earning. This way, they are saving for their retirement from an early age. Now, no money is too little. It's the little that will multiply over time, not the empty. Empty accounts don't multiply to anything. So, you don't need to wait until you start earning in thousands or millions before investing in your future.

It's good to invest in the global market from a young age because, truth be told, profits are not always guaranteed. The market for stocks and bonds and shares fluctuates from time to time due to the economy of the country you're trading with.

You need to have in mind that investment is a risk, especially long-term investments. However, when you start early, you will have gotten enough profit before you retire. Secondly, you must understand the global market better and make more informed investment decisions.

Now, know that in investment, the greater the risk, the greater the reward. The lesser the risk, the lesser the reward. That's why before investing in anything, ensure you research it properly. There are stories of ventures that started well but collapsed after a while, and people lost lots of money. So, ensure you have your facts right, especially if you wish to invest heavily.

The world has gone global, and you don't want to be left behind. Start researching areas where you can invest with your savings so your savings can generate more money for you.

Workbook 7

1. You have a week of free time during summer vacation. Design a schedule incorporating various learning forms, such as reading, taking an online course, and attending a workshop. Explain how this week of learning will benefit you.

2. You receive significant money as a gift for your 18th birthday. Discuss two different approaches you could take with this money: spending it all now on short-term desires or saving and investing it for long-term financial security.

3. You've been asked to give a presentation at school about a skill you recently acquired. Describe the skill, how you learned it, and its impact on your confidence and abilities.

Takeaway 7

Dear teen, as you strive for a better future, it's important to recognize the importance of self-investment. Learn as many marketable skills as possible, especially in your field of interest. This will boost your resume and marketability.

As you invest in yourself, also invest in financial assets, not only to satisfy your short-term needs but also your long-term needs. You can strike a balance between both through calculative investment.

As you go on, always seek advice before you make any investments. That's because the world is advancing technologically and has a great impact on the Investment world. You must understand your investments, or else you'll lose a lot of returns.

Chapter 8

Long-Term Financial Planning

"To achieve what 1% of the world's population has (Financial Freedom), you must be willing to do what only 1% dare to do...hard work and perseverance of the highest order.
– **Manoj Arora**

Goal-Oriented Investing for Teens

Everyone wants to make a little extra, but the workload is a hindrance. Investment allows you to make extra without really working. In investment, you use money to make money. The best part is there are no age limits to investing. As long as you have money to spare, you're in.

This means teens can be investors, whether they're minors or new adults (18 or 21, according to the country's customs). Though for minors, the investment will be in their names, but it'll be controlled by their parents/guardians till they're of age.

Nevertheless, as exciting as it is to invest and make money at a young age, there is a need to make goal-oriented investments. You can't just start investing because you hear it pays without having a goal for it.

If you do that (especially young adults who can control their investments), you'll lose more than you'll gain. Even when you gain, you may end up wasting the money on inconsequential things. That's because you don't have a plan on what to do with the returns and have little or no knowledge about investment.

After deciding to make investments, the first thing to do is set a goal. Write down what you want to use the money for and place those goals in order of priority.

For instance, as a teenager, you can invest to save up for college, add a percentage of your returns to the family income, buy a car, or help your friend pay their fees.

It's important you set goals so that once you start getting returns on your investment, you can channel the money to doing something reasonable.

After deciding what you want to do with the money, it's time to seek professional advice or research the best investments for teens. You need to learn a little about the market to make an informed decision.

When investing, consider your principal and calculate how much it'll generate at the end of the intended year of withdrawal. This will help you know whether you can meet your goal at the right time.

Since you may not have a steady source of income, you don't want to put your money in a risky investment even though the returns can snowball. Go for investments that are safe but promising, like cash or bonds.

Finally, after making your investment, keep a close watch. Investment is a risky venture. You win some and lose some or even lose all. So, it's not for the faint at heart.

Understanding the Power of Compounding

Whether you have a short-term or a long-term goal, you should go for an investment supporting the power of compounding. This way, you can achieve your goals at the time you planned.

You may ask, What is the power of compounding?

The power of compounding is generally defined as "interest upon interest", or interest-generating interest. In simple terms, it's when the interest in your principal is added to be your new principal and generates interest. As a new interest is added, the new amount becomes the new principal and continues like this throughout the compounding period.

For example: If your principal is $100,000, and your interest is $500, your return will be $100,500. This becomes your new principal, and when your next interest is added, it's added to both your principal and the interest. So you get $500 for your principal and an extra $50 for your old interest, making it a total of $101,550. This is how the interests will continue to generate interests for the period of your investment. So, at the end, you will earn more.

This is different from simple interest. In simple interest, your interests don't generate interest; only your principal does.

For example: If your principal is $100,000, and your interest is $500, your balance will be $100,500. When your next interest is added, it'll be $101,000. Interests will only be added to your principal.

The power of compounding is expressed with this formula:

$$= [P (1 + i)n] - P$$

$$= P [(1 + i)n - 1]$$

Where:

P = principal

i = annual interest rate

n = number of compounding periods

For example, calculate the compound interest if John invests $20,000, with an interest rate of 5% annually for 2 years.

$20,000 [(1+0.05)^2 -1 =

$20,000 [1.1025 - 1] =

$2050

Compound interest is difficult to calculate, and its returns are taxable. However, it helps you save more, meet your targets, make more investments, and helps you meet up with unforeseen bills.

The main idea of compound interest is compound period and frequency. That is, the time it takes for interests to be added and how frequently that addition is done. Interest frequency can be daily, monthly, quarterly, half-yearly, or annually.

It all depends on the plan you choose and your custodian. The more frequently your interests are added, the faster they'll grow. The power of compounding increases the speed at which your money grows.

Then again, withdrawing your interests before the stated years of investment will affect your final return. So, exercise patience when compounding. If you've planned to invest for 40 years, wait till then, even if it's more than the allowed withdrawal age.

The longer it stays, the more returns you'd have. So, start investing now. You can start with the little you have now, and it'll grow over the years.

The Importance of Asset Allocation

As the idiom goes, *Don't put all your eggs in one basket*. That's what asset allocation is all about. It's scattering your assets in equities, cash (and its equivalent), debts, fixed income, etc. This saves you a lot in the long run.

That's because investment is a risk of high loss or high rewards. It's an unpredictable market for even the experts. That's due to market volatility (fluctuation of value and prices). Imagine investing a chunk of money into stocks, hoping it'll generate a huge return because the market seems stable. But the tide turns, and your investment sinks. That's a big blow.

However, when you scatter your assets, irrespective of the market's volatility, you won't lose everywhere. For instance, if market volatility affects the value of equities, you may lose there, but you will gain in your bonds and cash investment.

Again, by allocating your assets, you can get higher returns and fewer losses. You can't lose in all areas because all assets grow at different paces. So if one drops, others will rise.

In addition, it helps you keep a check on your portfolio. When you notice one investment is increasing beyond your intention on your portfolio and another is not increasing as planned, you can sell off the excess of the first and invest in the other. This way, your portfolio is balanced and organized.

Asset allocation also enables you to beat your goals, especially short-term goals. If you need money urgently for something important, you can gather the profits from all your assets to settle the issue.

Consequently, multiple assets equal more interest, and this equals continuous investment. With asset allocation, you can reinvest your multiple interests into something else like self-development. Your assets will still continue to make more profits.

Furthermore, asset allocation allows you to decide on your investments due to your risk tolerance. If you're not a risk taker, you can invest 70% into bonds and cash and less on stocks and shares. Bonds and cash are less likely to fall, unlike stocks. The only difference is that the lower the risk, the lower the returns, and the higher the risk, the higher the returns.

The Role of Technology in Investing

Almost every sector today has benefited a lot from technology, and the investment sector is not left out. Technological advancements have made investing easy and more productive. It's almost always a win-win situation for investors.

To begin with, technology has increased investment awareness. With the advent of the internet came an influx of information on almost any topic, including investment. Before the internet came, you had to read newspapers or employ the services of a broker or an advisor to learn about investment.

But today, you just need access to the internet. You can find information about investment options, how to get started, the risks involved, and other vital information about investment. With this, you can decide whether to start or not. You'll also be equipped with a primary knowledge of investment before seeing an advisor if you wish to.

Secondly, technology has brought investments closer to us. All you need to start investing today is a smartphone or PC with an internet connection. With your phone, you can download apps and open a brokerage account.

On this platform, you'll find lots of investment options and information. This is unlike it was earlier. Earlier, you'd need to employ the services of a broker to help you invest. It takes a lot of money and time.

This tedious process made it difficult to start an investment for teens because even adults find it hard. It made a lot of people seek other reliable ways of saving for their future.

That's not the case today. Today, teens and adults can invest without the help of a middleman. It saves cost; it's faster and more efficient.

Thirdly, technology has greatly improved the chances of successful investments. Before now, getting a good return on investment was almost 40/60. There was a higher chance of loss than gain. Plus, you needed to go through a middleman, mostly a broker or banker, who had the knowledge of the market to invest on your behalf.

That's because only a few could read the volatility of the market. Even then, it still wasn't predictable and needed constant supervision to know exactly when to trade.

Since the reading was done manually, the chances of constant supervision (24/7) were slim. So people lost money, but they continued, depending on luck. And sometimes, they were indeed lucky.

But today, you don't need to watch your investments like a hawk. Technology has made some platforms, like financial planning software and others, available that can monitor your investments and even make predictions for you on the pattern of inflow and outflow of cash.

Since it's a machine that is doing the reading, it can always keep tabs on your investment. Also, algorithms and other AI automation have made calculating returns easy, fast, and accurate.

With all of these in place, it's easy to track your investments and even faster and cheaper to trade. Now, there's no middleman between you and your investments, so you save the cost of hiring one.

Aside from that, you're sure of your gains and losses. You no longer have to depend on what a middleman says. As you keep track of your investments, you will learn your mistakes and find ways to correct them. This way, you gain more experience and knowledge about the business.

Again, with technology, you have all the information you need about your investments at your fingertips. Investors today have little or no need to visit banks to obtain information about the progress of their investments or make complaints.

As an investor, you can link up with your advisor online for any advice or information you need. There's no need for appointments. This saves you time and resources.

Aside from communicating with an advisor, certain automation can filter the influx of information available online and highlight relevant information related to your interest using your search history. This means you don't have to spend all your time reading through all the information online.

It'll also aid you in making decisions quickly, as you have the information at the right time. You can also find better or new investment options online and be acquainted with any new information.

This way, you'll know when and how to invest. You will lose less and gain more. Some platforms can even give you relevant advice and suggestions on how and what to invest in. This will save you the stress of always consulting an advisor and save you the cost.

Moving on, technology has made asset allocation easy. Unlike in the past, when you had to invest in individual stocks for multiple income, an ETF provides that platform today. With Exchange-traded funds, you get to make multiple investments and diversify your portfolio.

Asset allocation is a sure way of getting returns. It's like not putting all your eggs in one basket. You get to invest in bonds, stocks, mutual funds, and other assets on a single platform. So, irrespective of how the market fluctuates, it won't all read the same.

If the value of one drops, there's a high chance that the other won't. So, one way or another, you are sure of getting a return, though some higher than others.

Another key addition of technology to the investment world is its security. You no longer have to be worried about being cheated by a middleman. Technology has provided ways to encrypt datasets.

You can be sure that your investments, transactions, and personal details are safe. There's a slim possibility of hacking. You just need to use strong passwords so it can be difficult to hack.

So far, technology has greatly improved the investment industry with all its inputs. The industry has witnessed tremendous growth, advancement, and an influx of investors over the years.

The Future of Work

With today's technological advancements, the question of the future of work is paramount. What will the workforce look like in the near future? Will companies need workers? Or are we all going to own a robot?

Indeed, no one can correctly predict the future of work, but we can deduce something from our past and present. For instance, in the past, if you wanted to travel, you would have to walk the distance or take a camel or mule. Companies needed many workers to do everything, from producing to manufacturing and packaging. The story has changed. Today, we have smartphones that can contact people even from another country. Today, large, fast, and efficient equipment does most of the work in companies.

We've seen that through the years, as technology advanced, the need for workers dropped. Companies needed fewer and fewer workers, especially as the equipment and machines were improved to do more.

Also, with the invention of AI and Automation, even some more equipment is no longer needed. Some industries are already making use of AI, while others are testing their capacity and how much they can drive them to do.

Now, with all these facts before our eyes, there is no doubt that the future of work is threatened. Humans are fast being displaced from the nation's workforce. It's also not surprising because machines do the work faster, better, more accurately, and more efficiently than humans can. That's because they are programmed, but humans are not. We're humans.

As technology advances, it is safe to say that the need for workers in organizations and institutions will drop drastically in the near future. In 2030, an estimated 12 million US workers (especially low-wage earners) are likely to shift jobs. (Ellingrud, Kweilin et al., 2023).

Somewhere soon, companies will be forced to go into remote working. They will begin to hire people with knowledge about the job, then those with certificates, because even today, interviews are conducted online.

Certain jobs like food services, customer care, and sales, may likely be replaced by AI or automation. The workers needed to work physically will be more of those in the medical field, transportation, and jobs that need physical contact.

Unlike humans, they don't feel weak or in pain. They are fast, efficient, and can do a whole lot in minutes than humans can do in hours. It'll be a welcome development, but everyone has to put in a little extra effort to stay useful.

Setting Up a Roth IRA

The future waits for no one. So, as long as you breathe every day, you need to invest in your future because one day, it'll come. As a teen, I don't have the I'm-too-young mentality. Your parents and grandparents were once teens. It's all a matter of time.

The question should be, how do you want to enjoy your retirement? Do you want to be strapped to others and be an inconvenience, or do you want to retire early and enjoy your days? It all depends on how well you invest in your retirement today.

As a teen, you can start saving for retirement by opening a Roth individual retirement account (IRA). The main requirement for whoever wants to open this account is a source of income. That means you need to have a job as a teen. That's because your TIN or SSN is required to open the account.

A Roth IRA is an individual retirement account that doesn't charge tax on your savings or final withdrawal, but you can only deposit as much as you earn, not more. For instance, if your salary is $100,000, you can deposit less but not more than that amount.

One benefit of opening a Roth IRA at a young age is having more time to save. If you're 19 and start saving $500, when you're 65, you'll have $23,000, aside from compound interests.

With this, you're sure that your retirement days will be fun. However, note that you can't withdraw until you're 59½.

To open a Roth IRA account, follow these easy steps:

- **Step 1:** Choose a reliable, efficient, and friendly custodian to open your Roth IRA. Some custodians are Fidelity Investments, Interactive Brokers, Fundraise, Vanguard, Betterment, TD Ameritrade, etc.

- **Step 2:** You'll be given a form to fill. To do this, you'll need your SSN or TIN, savings account number, your bank's routing transit number, any means of identification, the details of your employer, and finally, the details of your beneficiary (next of kin).

- **Step 3:** You need to make investment choices. Your Roth IRA isn't just where you save. It's an account with zero tax charges but allows you to invest in stocks, bonds, cash, etc. You have to choose what to invest, but I'd advise you to scatter your assets for higher returns.

- **Step 4:** Keep a close check of your investment. You can also set up a contribution scheme to transfer money from your account to the Roth IRA.

As you venture into the world of investment, you must consult experts to guide you into making the right investments for your age so you don't incur many losses.

Setting Up a Retirement Account

As a teen, it's time to start preparing for retirement. Not everyone will be privileged to get a government job. If you're working in a private organization, you need to start planning for your future to have a happy retirement.

Setting up a retirement account is easy, but you need a professional guide to help you make the right choices. For starters, you want to set a retirement target. To do this, consider when you want to retire and how much you'd like to have then.

If you can choose what you want to do after retirement (like pursuing a hobby or area of interest), you can research how much it'll take to do it. If you hope to go into experimentation, you should know it'll cost a lot.

All these factors will inform your decision on the principal you should start with. You don't have to get an accurate amount; you just need a rough estimate. There are retirement and compound interest calculators online you could use.

If you discover that you don't have up to the money you need to start with, you can wait a bit and save some more before you start investing. You don't want to fall short on your dreams because of small investments.

When you've decided on all the above factors, it's time to pick a custodian. You can start by inquiring about their retirement account options at your current bank. They will put you through the details.

However, in selecting a custodian, you need to determine their reputation. When you're okay with the reviews you've gotten, you can then find out if there's a fee to open the account and what they require. You should also ask about their accounts with the power of compounding.

Some reputable custodians include Fidelity Investments, Interactive Brokers, Fundraise, Vanguard, Betterment, TD Ameritrade, and JP Morgan. (Benson, 2023)

When you're sure of your custodian, the next step is to determine the kind of retirement account you want to open. You can go for the Roth IRA or brokerage account as a teen. As you grow older, you can go for the Traditional IRA, the 401(k) (for private workers), or the 403(k) (for government workers) plan.

Each of these has its merits and setbacks. Your financial advisor will give you a detailed explanation and suggest a suitable one. As an employer, maximize the provision of the 401(k) plan your company provides. It'll save you some cost.

Now, when you've decided on the retirement account to open, visit your custodian, fill out the form, and you're good to go.

Now that you've set up a retirement account, you need to seek professional advice and start investing. You shouldn't leave your account bare. Let it make more money for you.

Tax-Efficient Investing

Tax and investments are close relations. While it's true that tax is important and almost insignificant, it reduces your investments, and you may not meet your goal. It's therefore important to include tax rates in your investment plans.

However, there are ways of reducing tax on your investments. Some accounts are tax-free, tax-deferred, or tax-exempt, like Roth and Traditional IRA accounts, 401(k)s. These accounts can help you save money on tax or reduce the weight on your investment.

You may need to speak to a professional tax advisor as a teen. Your tax advisor will properly analyze and advise you on the type of investment to make and the type of account to use.

The tax-advantaged account, for instance, provides tax-deferred or tax-exempt investments. However, there are some limitations, like a specified time to withdraw and tax at the time of withdrawal for a tax-deferred account.

This is different from taxable accounts like a brokerage account. This account is taxed according to your tax bracket. However, it has few restrictions, and you can withdraw your returns anytime with no tax.

Seeking Professional Advice

You'll agree with me that it'll be unwise to jump into an investment simply because they promised it'll yield. If you've never invested before or you have, but you don't know the ropes, it's important you see a financial advisor.

A financial advisor serves as a counselor on financial matters. They are professionals in the field of investment, like the brokers and bankers. They understand how the market works and can give you professional advice on investing.

I know technology has made things easy, and you can do research online or watch videos. Still, you need to seek professional advice. Even if you got financial advice from a loved one, it's still necessary that you seek professional advice.

You see, non-professionals can only advise you based on what they've done that worked for them or what they've heard works. All of these are not facts. I tell you, you don't want to joke with your hard-earned money. Don't trust that advice and invest your money in an asset that yields at snail's speed or crashes completely.

On the other hand, professionals don't tell you what they think; they tell you what the fact is. They will analyze your goals or guide you in making one, your income, and your risk tolerance. After considering these factors, they will then advise you on the best and safest investments to make.

They will teach you how to monitor and trade, and set up a nice portfolio for you. Whenever you hit a roadblock, you can always seek their advice on maneuvering your way out of it. They do the research for you and weigh whatever information they get before sharing it.

The account is still yours, so you will be more in control. It's therefore important to make your own findings. However, whatever findings you make that want to lead you to a decision, ensure you run it by your advisor for confirmation.

This way, you get to make the right investments and reinvestments. The easiest way to find an advisor is to visit your bank or any bank. Ask them about their investment options. They'll refer you to a financial guide who will tell you everything you need.

If all they tell you is about their investment options, ask for advice on which to invest in. You can also request for a financial advisor. Sometimes their services aren't free, but it's very necessary to hear from one.

Creating a Long-Term Financial Plan

As a teen, you're not too young to create a long-term financial plan. In fact, this is the best time to make the plan so you can start executing it in time. A financial plan is a detailed plan on dividing and controlling your finances. A long-term financial plan focuses on making a financial plan that is future-specific.

This plan has to include your income, debts, insurance, tax, and investments. In making a long-term financial plan, first consider your current income. You're still young, so there's a high chance of shifting to a higher-paying job in the future, but for now, plan with what you have.

Regarding investment, no amount is too small or too great. Whatever you put in will yield something in return if you make wise investment choices. So, begin with what you have. If you're not okay with what you have, save up a bit before you start.

Next, find a division strategy that will work for you. Better still, you can go with the 50/30/20 budget principle. You use 50% of your income to offset debts and pay bills, 30% for your personal needs and pleasure, and then 20% goes for savings and investments.

However, suppose you live with your parents/guardians, and they feed, clothe, and foot your bills. In that case, you should apply this principle like this: 50% for savings and investments, 30% for personal needs and pleasure, and then 20% can be your contribution to the family or for philanthropic use.

But if you know that you don't have to touch your income to survive, then you can plan to invest 80% of your income instead. This way, you can plan to divide it and make several investments instead of one.

In the future, when you have your own family, you can revert this principle to the first application method. Also, your income will increase when you get a high-paying job. You can start up new investments and even consider investing in high-risk assets.

After breaking down your income, it's time to seek professional advice and choose the best kind of investment to make for a long-term purpose. You'll need to open a Roth IRA. This will help save you tax on your investments because it's tax-free. Scatter your assets so you can be sure of always getting returns.

In investing, choose a custodian that offers compounding interest on your investments. Ensure you make and follow a portfolio. As you make your plan, you need to plan for emergencies and large debts.

Financial plans are not once-in-a-lifetime plans. They are: You need to review them occasionally as you welcome a change. For instance, if you made the plan at 18, you'll need to review it when you switch jobs or get a higher-paying job. You also need to follow its progress report.

If your returns are not up to the figure in your plan after five years, you need to find ways of making it meet up. Speak to your financial advisor or do some research. Your financial plan serves as your financial guide. On the other hand, if your investments have overshadowed your financial plan, you can amend it.

You need to avoid accruing debts for your future financial plan to come to fruition. Ensure you live even beneath your means, and never use or reduce your savings. In fact, once you set it aside, don't consider it your money anymore.

Workbook 8

1. Imagine you have $1,000 to invest. Create a hypothetical asset allocation plan, distributing the funds between stocks, bonds, and cash. Explain your choices.

2. Share a financial goal for your future, whether it's buying a car, traveling, or saving for college. How can goal-oriented investing help you achieve this goal?

3. Calculate the potential growth of a Roth IRA investment over 20 years, assuming a certain rate of return. Compare this to a regular savings account. How does the Roth IRA offer a significant advantage?

Takeaway 8

Now you know that no time is too early to start planning for retirement. The earlier you start, the more gains you'll accrue. It's time to make a long-term financial plan to be relevant in the future.

As you begin your journey of long-term financial investment, seek professional advice on the right account to open, how to open it, and the right investments to make. You want to go for tax-efficient investments to enable you to save more.

Make your investments grow faster by using the power of compounding on your returns. When you save for retirement, the fear of retirement will dissipate. As long as you have a source of income, open a Roth IRA today to secure a better future.

Chapter 9

Building a Legacy of Wealth

"We build our legacy piece by piece, and maybe the whole world will remember you or maybe just a couple of people, but you do what you can to make sure you're still around after you're gone.
– David Lowery

Giving Back

Sophia Killingbeck is a 9-year-old girl. At age 4, she was critically ill and was admitted to the Children's Hospital of Michigan. She was so ill that she couldn't do anything herself. She couldn't see, understand anything, or speak. She spent the whole summer of that year in the hospital.

After that period, she recovered and was discharged. After her recovery, Sophia began to donate truckloads of toys to the children at the hospital every summer. This has put a lot of smiles on the faces of the children.

When asked why she donates truckloads of toys to the hospital, she replied, "Every time I got a present, I felt like I wasn't alone." (DeGiulio & Clarke, 2021)

Sophia is just one out of many who have found a way to give back to their society in their own little way. Giving back to society is simply helping and empowering people around you to be better.

Sophia's story also shows that no law prohibits you from giving back to society as a teen.

I know that you'll want to ask how? Or, With what? Well, you don't need to be a millionaire before you can empower the people around you. There are so many ways you can give back to society.

For one, if you have wealthy parents, you can solicit their assistance and support orphanages with cash, food items, clothes, etc. If you can't reach everyone at an orphanage, you can seek your parents' help to pay a less privileged friend's fees. It can be at school or a neighbor.

You can also decide to bake cookies or brownies for seniors in nursing homes. You can keep them company, read them a story, or make them laugh. You don't have to go every day. Once or twice a week is enough.

Giving back doesn't have to be something big or public. It just has to make people happy and feel loved. It's about saying a kind word to someone who's depressed, giving a piece of bread to a beggar with a smile, and generally showing love to people, especially those who need it.

At school or the office, you can spot that loner or someone who's always sad, and be their friend. You can organize free tutorials for junior high students. Also, you can lend a helping hand to people who need it. You're impacting lives and spreading love.

In addition, you can offer volunteer services. Join a volunteer team that interests you. It can be those into community service or those who cook and serve people in shelters. If you can't do it alone, you can talk to three or more of your friends and share the idea. Get them to join you and put smiles on people's faces the best way you know how.

Giving back to society is looking beyond yourself and seeing others. It's realizing we're all humans, some richer than others, but still humans. It's thinking of others and their well-being. It's adding happiness and kindness to this grieving world.

Giving back to society makes you feel good about yourself, relevant, kind, and happy. You feel a special kind of fulfillment and satisfaction when someone says, Thank you, to you, or you see people laughing because of you. It feels really good to make others feel good.

Teaching Others

Teaching is a tradition that is as old as man. In ancient times, a people's history was passed down by word of mouth. In some cultures, it was coined and told as a story. In some others, it was sung.

All of these were to make it hard to forget. But as time went on, information became varied. People began to research various fields, and new information multiplied and transcended the border of ethnicity. To top it off was the advent of digital devices that encouraged communication.

As a result, the community began to grow into a digital one, seeking knowledge in various fields to fit into the changing world. This led people to read and master various courses and transfer the knowledge by teaching others.

Ever since, knowledge has continued to grow, and the need for teachers keeps increasing. In schools today, certain students easily understand their fellow students' explanations more than their teachers.

This encouraged students to teach their peers. And as the saying goes, givers never lack, so also students who teach others never run out of knowledge. In fact, they gain more than they give at the end of the day.

There are lots of benefits accrued to teaching others. Let's look at this example.

Percy is very good at math. His report card always carries 100% or at least 95%. However, his friends, Penny and Jake, never go above 50% in math. However, among the three of them, Penny is more knowledgeable in geography, but Percy is terrible at it.

Percy has an idea and proposes that he'd teach them math while Penny will teach them geography. At the end of that term, they all do well in both subjects.

Teaching others can build your confidence, self-esteem, and leadership abilities. Like the saying goes, knowledge is power. When you have knowledge and can dispense it correctly, there's a kind of power and self-confidence that builds in you.

You'll feel more confident talking to people, and you won't easily feel intimidated by the potential in others. It makes you feel valuable and relevant. It increases your self-worth. It'll be hard for you to look down on yourself because you know you have what others don't.

Even in class, it'll boost your morale when answering questions. The more answers you get, the greater your confidence is being boosted. So, teaching others makes you feel good about yourself.

Aside from that, teaching others makes you a better learner. You get better in the subject you're teaching because you recite it from time to time. It sharpens your memory and keeps the information evergreen. As you teach others and learn more by doing so, you're practicing what is called, the Protégé effect. It means understanding better by preparing, practicing, or teaching others. (Granger, 2019).

Furthermore, the more you teach others, the more you'll want to know. The more you know, the broader your knowledge gets. When you teach others, you want to read ahead and broadly. You won't glance over the course but do in-depth research to understand what you intend to teach correctly.

This is because you wouldn't want any form of embarrassment, like not being able to answer a question your students ask. You wouldn't want to get stuck while teaching because you can't explain that area. In doing so, you're expanding your knowledge on that subject, and you'd be a master in it in no time.

Again, when you teach others, you will definitely pass your exams. It'll also make learning in class easy for you. That's because you may be ahead of the teacher while striving to meet up with your students. So when your teacher comes to teach that topic, it'll just be additional knowledge.

With this wealth of knowledge and a constant recollection of it, you can do well in exams or even pop quizzes. In the end, you'll come out with an excellent result.

Teaching others also affords you the opportunity to raise people. You'll get to see your students progress from zero to hundreds. That's the joy of every teacher. You'll help build lives, increasing their chances of becoming better persons.

It'll also increase the respect you get from your peers and even teachers. Everyone will hold you in high esteem, and you'll bring joy to your family.

On the other hand, you may not teach a subject. It may be showing a new basketballer the ropes. Or it may be teaching a friend to bake a cake or make cookies. It can be helping newbies in the cheerleading team get their parts.

You can just teach others something you're very good at. Don't ever think you're good at nothing. That's just your head telling you what you want to hear to keep you in your comfort zone. Whatever you love doing, you should teach someone interested in learning.

However, some people are timid and fidget whenever they are in front of others. If you're in this category but want to teach others and benefit from its benefits, there are ways to go about it.

For one, you can start from home. Start with your younger ones or neighbors' kids. You can all gather under a tree or at the back of the house and teach them whatever subjects they find difficult. When you've had enough practice, it'll build confidence in you, and you can go further to teaching your peers.

If you don't have anyone around to practice with, you can join a club. Any club of your choice. It's about building confidence to stand before people and do something. So when you join the club, try to be active in whatever you're all involved in. If it's a debate club, motivate yourself to take on debates. As you do this, you'll build your confidence.

Another way you can face your fears is to practice before a mirror or before a friend in private. Or, you can start answering or asking questions in class. This will also build your confidence and expose you. When you answer correctly consecutively, your peers will see you as intelligent. That's an opening. When you make a tutorial open, they'll come.

Teaching others lets you know your strengths and weaknesses. It boosts your morale and popularity. It also strengthens your cognitive and metacognitive abilities. It sharpens your communication and leadership skills.

The Power of Networking

Never underestimate the power of networking. Networking is interacting and creating a relationship with like-minded people to reach a personal goal. It's about meeting and associating with new people, either for professional or social purposes.

Networking can be done for various purposes. Professional networking involves consciously associating and communicating with like-minded people in your profession. Your aim can be to create relationships you know will benefit you soon, get a link to a job opportunity, or strike a business proposal on friendly ground.

In trying to network professionally, you'll have to attend business meetings/dinners, join a professional community online or offline, and reach

out to those ahead of you in your field online like on LinkedIn. You'll need to make some friends, acquaintances, and some other mentors.

In this kind of networking, especially when you have a specific goal, you have to put in conscious effort. You can research those high fliers in your field, study their profile and follow them on their social media platforms. You can send an email stating who you are and what you want.

Your first approach shouldn't involve stating your proposal. Remember, you're not just going for the business today; you want to establish a relationship that will fetch you more in the future. So, you should first build a relationship. You can start by appreciating one of their works that you have probably read about. This will get them talking and leave an impression about you in their mind.

However, in relating with other professionals, ensure you have something to offer, too. That's very important. You don't want them to see you as a beggar or a parasite. You need to have something they want and present it in a way that makes it seem like they can't have it anywhere else. It needs to be unique. That's your bait.

When they see you have worth, they'll feel interested in whatever relationship you're trying to create. At the first meeting, preferably at a business dinner or gathering, you can introduce yourself and what you do. Then, try to get their business card. Remember, before going in, you must know who the person is and how they can help you.

The plan is not to gather business cards of all the wealthy people. It's to get business cards that will help you reach your goals. When you get the card, make the call. It should be an informal call just to register your presence. After that, let it be till you have something important to offer or propose.

Many people have gotten jobs they never knew were open due to professional networking. Aside from that, you can choose mentors from them. This way, you'll garner knowledge and become better in your field. So, professional networking is crucial for growth and advancement in your profession.

Aside from professional networking, you can go into social networking. This is about meeting new people and starting new relationships. It's more informal. This is especially beneficial for timid individuals who want to break out of their shells.

Creating social networks links you to many people and exposes you to what's happening around you. To get started, you can join a volunteer team or book club and attend carols and other community-organized gatherings. Now, if you're the shy type, going alone won't help because you will end up not talking to anyone.

So, if you really want to socialize, go with a friend who is the queen of socializing. Your friend will make you talk to people, and that way, you will get to meet new people, and before you know it, you're a social bee yourself.

However, if you think this is too much exposure, you can do online networking. Search for people you love for their work and follow them on social media platforms. Send and accept reasonable friend requests. Go through their previous posts, and if you love what they do, strike up a conversation starting with your thoughts about their work. This way, you'll make lots of reasonable and helpful connections.

The best part of online networking is that your choices aren't limited to people in your locality alone. You can reach out to anyone anywhere in the world.

Creating a Family Investment Strategy: Involving Parents and Siblings

Now that you know the importance of investment and its benefits, you can introduce your family to it. You can create an investment strategy to help you make the right choices. An investment strategy guides you into making the right investments to help you achieve your goals at the appointed time.

It contains what to do, how to do it, why you should do it, and the end result of doing or not doing it. It should also contain emergency options or alternatives if one strategy doesn't work.

You don't have to do this yourself. You should call your family together, sell the vision to them, and tell them the benefits. You all can then take it up as a family project. Do research together and draw up investment strategies together.

There are quite several strategies you can use for a family investment. Firstly, you can plan to open a brokerage, Roth IRA, or 401(k) account. This will be easy for your parents to open. In fact, you all should open one each if you meet the criteria. That's a good strategy to save for your future. The earlier you start, the more returns you'll get.

Some of these accounts are tax-free, and you can make multiple investments in them. You should choose an investment that will pay well, like stocks. It's true stocks are highly risky, but if you're saving for retirement and diligent in following the market, you might hit a jackpot before the investment period elapses.

Then again, you want to be on the safe side, so you should balance it. If you are five in your family, the account of the last two can be used to purchase the stocks. They have lots of years ahead of them. Then, you can invest in bonds, ETFs, Mutual funds, and so on with other people's accounts. This way, you don't lose out.

Another investment strategy is the growth investment. There are lots of new companies springing up here and there. You can keep an eye out for one or do research about them. When you do, list those that you feel have both present and future relevant goods and services to offer.

When you're sure of your list, you can then invest in them. It's a risky

investment because it's 50/50. They are upcoming, so they may rise high, not too high, or collapse completely. However, if they rise high, you'll

Building a Legacy of Wealth

have hit a jackpot because you'll grow with them. So, this strategy is better applied when you have money to spare.

Again, there's the buy-and-hold investment. This strategy is about buying shares or other assets when they are undervalued, and then you don't sell till their value rises. It's like buying something at $5 and selling at $50 because it's in immediate demand.

There's also active investment. One of you can decide to learn the art of reading the market and following it up. The active investment means one of you needs to follow up on investments to monitor which is in vogue. When you identify the ones the market favors at that time, you invest in them. This kind of strategy needs constant checking.

Lastly, you can open a trust fund or life insurance. This way, you will save money for everyone's future in case of any eventualities. But when doing this, be clear and specific on who owns what to avoid conflict at the end of the day.

In making family investment strategies, think long-term more than short-term. That's because you need to consider the children's education, retirement for both parents, owning your own place and car, a dream family vacation, and emergencies.

All of these should inform your investment choices. If you're not so buoyant, you shouldn't start with high-risk investments. Although it'll pay more, it's not worth it. You want to start with something safe and reliable.

Evolving as an Investor

Evolving as an investor means transcending from one level to another through careful observance and application of improved theory. It's supposed to happen as it lifts you from where you are to where you want to be.

As an investor, you need to evolve, that is, reflect, restrategize, and become more formidable. You can't keep doing the same thing you've been doing for years and expect a different result. There should come a point in your investment journey when you take time to stock your investments.

In evolving, you want to analyze each of your investments. Take note of the day it started, the goal you had for it, how long it should take to reach that goal, and how well it is growing. Take inventory of the ones that have exceeded their target and those lagging behind.

Also, look at the market and find out what's working now and how your investments can grow beyond what they are at the time. Check for new information on the market or new/better investment opportunities.

When you analyze your investment and find the issues, seek ways to solve them. If your investments are growing well, still seek improved ways to boost them. For instance, if you were investing on simple interest, you can improve the power of compounding. This way, your returns grow at an accelerated pace.

As you make your analysis, you want to reflect on your mistakes and losses. Try to pinpoint where you're lacking, what you're lacking in, and why. This will help you plan a new way forward. In your plan, think of all the things that could happen in the future and make a list. Then, think of ways to tackle or avoid those predictions.

If, after your analysis, you don't see anything wrong, but your investments are not growing well, then seek professional help. When you interact with another experienced investor or advisor, they can help analyze your assets and marketing strategies.

They'll then pinpoint areas that won't work or need a change. They'll tell you what to do and how to go about it. If you can't monitor your investment, it's better you entrust it to an AI or automation software. There are lots of them that can do the job.

Your evolution as an investor is like retreating to gather an arsenal that will help you overcome when you make a rebound. Don't just leave your investments as they were from day one. Always seek ways to improve. Seek ways to diversify your assets, and learn the market well to make more gains. The aim of investment is not just to have a name among those who have investments but to actually profit maximally from it.

Overcoming Adversity: Learning from Investment Mistakes

Mistakes are a natural phenomenon. I believe its original purpose is to reflect a wrong way of doing something so you can find the right way of doing it. Mistakes aren't meant to keep you down and out.

At one time or another, we've all failed at something. For instance, I doubt if anyone took their first step as a baby without falling. There's a possibility that you can fail at something, but failure doesn't mean that thing doesn't work.

Failure also doesn't mean you're not good enough or that there's no reason to try again. No. There are countless people, like Thomas Edison, who failed so many times but never gave up. The truth is, if someone is doing it, then it can be done. If you're not getting it right, it doesn't simply mean you're missing something out. This is how you should view your investment mistakes and failures. Don't capitalize on them and stop investing. That will be saying goodbye to a better future and the nice things of life.

As you go on in your investment journey, you are bound to make mistakes and incur losses. You can even make an obvious mistake probably because you weren't paying attention or because of misinformation. It will hurt, but it shouldn't end your investment journey. Instead of focusing on your mistakes and feeling low about them, why not learn from them? Firstly, you need to come to terms with the fact that you've made a mistake. Once you've accepted that fact, the next thing you should look out for is how to fix it.

Don't spend time grieving over a mistake without first looking for ways to remedy the situation. Once you notice a mistake, reach out to your financial advisor. Be sure there's nothing you can do before you conclude on the mistake.

If there's no remedy after your consultation and research, then learn from it. Learning from it isn't just about registering it in your mind to avoid it in the future. Not really. You need to analyze the mistake and see why it's a mistake and what should have been done.

Find out if it failed because you didn't keep a close watch, or because you didn't trade at the right time, or that investment wasn't the right call at that time. From that one mistake, dig out other possible loopholes that could have occurred. See how many mistakes and successes could have come out of that one mistake. That is, see all the ways it could have been a success and all the ways it could have still failed.

When you keep a record of these things with every mistake and seek advice on them, you'll become a success sooner than later.

So, don't make investment choices based on how you feel or what you've heard worked for someone else. You need to do proper research and be very sure before you invest.

As you continue to invest, don't give room for mistakes, but then again, expect it. When it comes (because it happens to even professionals), embrace it as a means of growing. Like the saying goes, *What doesn't kill you can only make you stronger*. Salvage what's left of your mistakes, learn from them, avoid them, and move on. Look ahead to all the wonderful benefits that will still come, and keep investing.

Identifying and Maximizing Opportunities for Wealth Creation

Wealth creation means discovering ways of making more money. In our world today, people miss out on rare opportunities because they weren't prepared to take them. You should always be prepared for opportunities that will open ways for wealth creation.

Sometimes, you need to source for these opportunities as regards the preparations you've already made. For instance, if you've saved up some money, you can seek investment opportunities. Again, if you have acquired a certain skill, you can keep your ears open for someone looking to learn or hire. Once you find it, grab the opportunity to teach or work. You'll earn money both ways.

So you see, opportunities abound, but only the prepared and disciplined are considered. Furthermore, in seeking opportunities, you need to have a goal in mind. You need to know what you want to achieve and to what magnitude. Only then can you define the opportunities you need and seek them.

For instance, if you want to be an inventor and the goal is to invent something exceptional one day, you know your goal cannot be achieved in a small place. You need a reputable and wealthy company for that. But then, how do you get there?

Now, you're not looking for an opportunity or waiting for it to come. You want to create it yourself. What you'll do is to get publicity. If I may ask, how many people around you know you as an inventor? In fact, do your family members even know?

Now, you need publicity. You can get this by inventing something as a project at school. If you're not in school, you can show it off at a community gathering. When you do this repeatedly, you've created opportunities for yourself. People will know who you are and what you can do. You may even get referrals from people you don't know.

Now, that's one. However, the goal is a reputable company. So, you keep striving. Next, you want to make something reasonable and distinct for presentation to the company. You can contact them by sending an email to request an audience. Or you can try to befriend a worker in that company so you have an inside man.

This way, when you get your audience, ensure you blow their mind. They may not hire you immediately, but you've etched your name in their hearts, and that's something positive.

This, however, doesn't mean you can't accept the offers of small companies. You should because they'll be a foundation for growing and gaining experience, but never remove your mind from the goal.

My point is that you prepare for opportunities that are in line with your area(s) of interest. Secondly, have a goal in mind. When the opportunity comes, grab it. If it hasn't come yet, look for it. If you can't find it, then create it. These opportunities will lead you on your journey to creating wealth for a better future.

Celebrating Financial Freedom: Enjoying the Fruits of Your Investing Labor

There's a saying that goes, *What you sow is what you'll reap.* It simply means if you sow nothing, you'll reap nothing. But for those who sow, the time of reaping is always exciting. It makes you forget the pain of the years of toiling and sowing.

The year of reaping is when you begin to eat the fruit of your labor. It's when you get to confidently pay for that car, complete the payment for the house, or go for a vacation you've only dreamed of till then. The joy of reaping spurs people to sow.

So it is at the end of your investment. When it's time to withdraw, you'll be smiling at the bank. At this point, you may be an adult or even a senior, but you're sure you can still chase your dreams. You're sure you're not a liability to anyone.

It's the time when you withdraw your savings of 20, 40, or even 50 years. It all depends on when you started saving. The earlier you start, the more gains ahead. That's why it's important you start saving for long-term goals as early as necessary.

Someone who saves for 55 years will have more than someone who saves for 20 years. However, it's still better to start investing now because a small return will always be better than no return.

Imagine that one of your short-term goals was to get a car, and you saved your investments for 3-5 years. Now, the time for withdrawal is here, and you withdraw your money. You'll feel rewarded and proud of yourself when you get the car. That's eating the fruit of your labor.

Again, imagine, after leaving your investments for 40 years from age 18, and now you're retiring. Imagine the amount you'd have as a retiree. Imagine doing all the things you planned to do after retirement with it. That's the satisfaction of investment.

When you make investments, you can determine when you want to retire. Imagine retiring at age 55. You still have years to do whatever your heart desires and have the money to fulfill those desires. That's plus the fact that you're still strong enough to do them and actually enjoy them.

Also, as you grow, you have peace of mind as regards the future. You can confidently talk about the future that most people see as the unknown world that should be avoided. You won't be scared of rainy days because you're prepared for them.

In fact, you have peace of mind knowing you have your money reading and generating more money. You see, not having money is enough frustration. But with your investments, even if things aren't going well with you, you'll still have hope. All these are the benefits you stand to gain when you sow into the investment world.

So you don't have to wait till you withdraw your investment before you start enjoying the fruit of your labor. You begin to enjoy some benefits just by starting up an investment.

Furthermore, you'll have multiple streams of income. This means more money to meet more needs. This is what some people term financial freedom. Some others see it as having money whenever it's needed, while others see it as having more than enough money to lavish as you please.

Whatever your definition, it all involves having money and making investments that can bring your financial freedom goal to fruition. You never have to depend on others, and you still get to have what you want.

So, as you invest today, think of your future. Picture in your mind's eye the day of withdrawal and getting that thing you've always wanted. This will keep you on your feet. Remember, only those who sow into investment will reap happy returns.

Workbook 9

1. Imagine you have $10,000 to invest, but you're not sure where to start. Describe a process you would follow to identify and evaluate investment opportunities.

2. Share a personal or observed example of an investment mistake. What went wrong, and what lessons did you or the person involved learn from the experience?

3. Pretend you're advising a friend who just experienced a significant investment loss. What advice and strategies would you offer to help them recover and avoid similar mistakes in the future?

Takeaway 9

It's necessary that you give back a part of all you've got to society. It's not a means of looking good or a course for pride. It's a philanthropic gesture that empowers others and helps them rise to be better people who can then give back to society. This way, you're making society a better place.

Aside from giving, at this point, you need to sit back and take an inventory of your investments. Highlight your mistakes over the years and all you could have done better. If possible, predict future mistakes to avoid. As you invest, get your family involved so you all can dream of financial freedom together.

Never give up on your investments because you'll eat the fruit of your labor at the end of the day. You'll get to buy that house, or that car, or go to that college, and live a nice life after retirement.

Conclusion

In the world of investors, there's a man who stands out, and his name is Raymond Thomas Dalio. He made his first unsure investment at 12 and has never looked back. Today, he is the co-CEO of Bridgewater Associates, a company he founded in 1975 that has never stopped making majestic waves in the investment world.

He was born in New York City, U.S., on the 8th of August 1949, to a jazz musician, Marino Dallolio. He lived a humble life and did odd jobs while growing up. At age 12, he ventured into caddying for people and did so for some wealthy people. That was when he heard about investing. He decided to try it out and used the $300 he had saved from caddying to buy shares of Northeast Airlines.

It was a risky investment because the airline was at the edge of bankruptcy but later merged with another company. When this happened, his investment tripled, which was the motivation he needed. That motivation led him to make other investments. There were some losses but more gains. He worked in different finance companies till he branched off and started Bridgewater in his apartment.

Bridgewater wasn't a success at first and had to be shut down, but later on, it thrived. Today, it has become a multibillion-dollar company. Raymond Dalio has awards to his name and has written some books about investment.

Here are some of his achievements:

- In 2012, Time 100 listed him as one of the 100 most influential people in the world.

- That same year, he held the rank of the second richest on the Rich List of Institutional Investor's Alpha.

- In 2015, Forbes's estimation of his net worth made him the second wealthiest hedge fund manager.

- As of 2022, he was the 123rd richest person in the world as Bloomberg News estimated his net worth as $15.7 billion.

Now, here's the thrilling aspect of his life. Dalio suffered from Barrett's esophagus but didn't let that deter him.

Secondly, he started Dalio Foundation to give back to society. He partners with schools, communities, and NGOs to empower young people and support them to do meaningful things in their lives.

Dalio began his investment journey as a teenager, and despite the hurdles he faced, he never stopped. In the end, his decision and determination paid off. Today, he's a multibillionaire and a husband and father. He has enough and gives back to society to raise young, ambitious, focused people.

This book has been an amazing journey so far, filled with loads of ideas to implement. Know that you can do what you've read. They're not difficult. You just need to put your mind to it like Dalio. Your results may or may not be as dramatic as Dalio's, but you get what I mean.

I'm happy for you if you've read to this point. However, investments will not invest themselves. That little money you've saved, invest it wisely. You don't have to spend it on getting that dress. You can always get more dresses if you invest the money. It'll bring in more money and help you secure a future you don't yet see.

With your investments, you will always have money to meet your needs, and I promise you that you'll enjoy the fruit of a long investment when it's time

for withdrawal. You just need to leave it for as long as possible.

Remember, it's only the investment you make now that you can withdraw later. Don't think you're too late or too early. Yes, right now is the perfect time to start if you haven't. If you have, kudos. Now, use the principles you've learned in this book and build your investment.

Lastly, please! Tell a friend about this book if you enjoyed it and please leave a review on Amazon to help other readers make an informed decision when deciding on what book could help in a powerful way!

Thank you!

References

Banton, C. (2022). How to Read the Psychological State of the Market with Technical Indicators. Investopedia. https://www.investopedia.com/articles/trading/03/010603.asp

Barber, B. M., & Odean, T. (2000). Trading Is Hazardous to Your Wealth: The Common Stock Investment Performance of Individual Investors. The Journal of Finance, 55(2), 773-806.

Beers, B. (2021). A Look at Primary and Secondary Markets. Investopedia. https://www.investopedia.com/investing/primary-and-secondary-markets/

Benson, Alana. "14 Best IRA Accounts of December 2021." *NerdWallet*, 31 Aug. 2023, www.nerdwallet.com/best/investing/ira-accounts.

Berger, R. (2014, April 30). Top 100 Money Quotes of All Time. Forbes. https://www.forbes.com/sites/robertberger/2014/04/30/top-100-money-quotes-of-all-time/

Bieber, C. (2020, June 8). 4 Carlos Slim Quotes That Are More Relevant to Investors Than Ever. The Motley Fool. https://www.fool.com/investing/2020/06/08/carlos-slim-quotes-are-more-relevant-investors.aspx

Brown, L. (2018). The Snowball Effect: How Compound Interest Grows Your Wealth. Financial Growth Magazine, 22(4), 18-22.

Brown, L. (2020). Growing Wealth: A Teen's Introduction to Money Management. Financial Youth Magazine, 19(3), 8-13.

Chen, J. (2023). Real Estate: Definition, Types, How to Invest in It. Investopedia. https://www.investopedia.com/terms/r/realestate.asp

Clarke, Kim DeGiulio, Kayla. "9-Year-Old Girl Helps Collect, Deliver Toys to Children's Hospital of Michigan." *WDIV*, 27 July 2021, www.clickondetroit.com/news/local/2021/07/27/9-year-old-girl-helps-collect-deliver-toys-to-childrens-hospital-of-michigan/. Accessed 2 Sept. 2023.

Dunn, E. W., Gilbert, D. T., & Wilson, T. D. (2011). If money doesn't make you happy, then you probably aren't spending it right. Science, 1643-1645.

Dunn, E. W., Gilbert, D. T., & Wilson, T. D. (2011). If money doesn't make you happy, then you probably aren't spending it right. Science, 1643-1645.

Ellingrud, Kweilin, et al. "Generative AI and the Future of Work in America | McKinsey." *Www.mckinsey.com*, 26 July 2023, www.mckinsey.com/mgi/our-research/generative-ai-and-the-future-of-work-in-america.

Fi.Money. (2023, August 22). What Are the 3 Major US Stock Exchanges? Fi.Money. https://fi.money/blog/posts/what-are-the-3-major-us-stock-exchanges

Fitzsimmons, D. (2021, July 29). Robinhood and the rise of teenage stock investors. Financial Markets News | Al Jazeera. https://www.aljazeera.com/economy/2021/7/29/robinhood-and-the-rise-of-teenage-stock-investors

Floyd, D. (2023). 10 Common Effects of Inflation. Investopedia. https://www.investopedia.com/articles/insights/122016/9-common-effects-inflation.asp

Folger, Jean. "Tax-Efficient Investing: A Beginner's Guide." *Investopedia*, 4 May 2023, www.investopedia.com/articles/stocks/11/intro-tax-efficient-investing.asp.

Granger, Brigitte. "The Protégé Effect: How Doing for Others Makes Us Do More." *Supporti*, 14 Aug. 2017, www.google.com/amp/s/www.getsupporti.com/amp/protege-effect-doing-for-others. Accessed 3 Sept. 2023.

Hayes, A. (2022). Technical Analysis: What It Is and How to Use It in Investing. Investopedia. https://www.investopedia.com/terms/t/technicalanalysis.asp

Horrigan, John B. "Lifelong Learning and Technology." *Pew Research Center: Internet, Science & Tech*, Pew Research Center: Internet, Science & Tech, 22 Mar. 2016, www.pewresearch.org/internet/2016/03/22/lifelong-learning-and-technology/.

In October 2022, consumer prices increased by 6.2% year on year - Informations rapides - 286 | Insee. (n.d.). https://www.insee.fr/en/statistiques/6653900

Johnson , Dave. "Redirect Notice." *Www.google.com*, 19 Nov. 2019, www.google.com/amp/s/www.businessinsider.com/obsolete-technology-examples-past-20-years-2019-11%3famp. Accessed 1 Sept. 2023.

Johnson, K. (2015, April 21). 14 Quotes to Get Inspired For Business Growth and Leadership. Black Enterprise. https://www.blackenterprise.com/15-quotes-inspire-business-growth-leadership/

References

Johnson, M. (2020). Tax Implications of Short-Term vs. Long-Term Investments. Taxation Today, 55(7), 14-20.

Kahneman, D., & Tversky, A. (1979). Prospect Theory: An Analysis of Decision under Risk. Econometrica, 47(2), 263-292.

Knutson, B., Adams, C. M., Fong, G. W., & Hommer, D. (2001). Anticipation of increasing monetary reward selectively recruits nucleus accumbens. Neuron, 30(1), 2001.

Knutson, B., Adams, C. M., Fong, G. W., & Hommer, D. (2001). Anticipation of increasing monetary reward selectively recruits nucleus accumbens. Neuron, 30(1), 2001.

Manyika, James, et al. "Jobs Lost, Jobs Gained: What the Future of Work Will Mean for Jobs, Skills, and Wages." *McKinsey & Company*, 2017, www.mckinsey.com/featured-insights/future-of-work/jobs-lost-jobs-gained-what-the-future-of-work-will-mean-for-jobs-skills-and-wages.

Markowitz, H. M. (1952). Portfolio selection. The Journal of Finance, 7(1), 77-91.

Miranda, Nicola. "The Impact of Illiteracy and the Importance of Early Intervention - World Literacy Foundation." *World Literacy Foundation*, 23 July 2021, worldliteracyfoundation.org/early-intervention-reduces-illiteracy/.

Moskowitz, D. (2023). The 10 Richest People in the World. Investopedia. https://www.investopedia.com/articles/investing/012715/5-richest-people-world.asp

Ramakrishnan, Manasa. "Lifelong Learning: What Is It All about and Why Should You Know about It?" *Emeritus Online Courses*, 15 Feb. 2022, emeritus.org/blog/benefits-of-lifelong-learning/#:~:text=Lifelong%20learning%20is%20broadly%20defined.

Smith, A. (2018). The Power of Compound Interest: Why It Pays to Start Investing Young. Financial Journal, 45(3), 22-31.

Smith, J., & Jones, A. (2019). The Impact of Early Investing on Future Wealth. Journal of Youth Finance, 15(3), 45-58.

Smith, J., & Taylor, A. B. (2012). The Effects of an Unstable Income on Psychological Well-Being: Implications of Fluctuating Incomes. International Journal of Stress Management, 19(4), 324-347.

Smith, J., & Taylor, A. B. (2012). The Effects of an Unstable Income on Psychological Well-Being: Implications of Fluctuating Incomes. International Journal of Stress Management, 19(4), 324-347.

Smith, J., et al. (2018). The Role of Information in Real Estate Investment. Journal of Property Research, 35(3), 277-294. DOI: 10.1080/09599916.2018.1435427

Smith, J. (2020). The Historical Average Annual Returns of the U.S. Stock Market. The Balance.

Statista. (2023, August 30). Largest stock exchange operators worldwide 2023, by market cap of listed companies. https://www.statista.com/statistics/270126/largest-stock-exchange-operators-by-market-capitalization-of-listed-companies/

Team, W. (2023). Real Estate Investing. WallStreetMojo. https://www.wallstreetmojo.com/real-estate-investing/

Thaler, R. (2015). Misbehaving: The Making of Behavioral Economics. W. W. Norton & Company.

Trends, Market. "5 Ways Technology Has Improved Investments." *Analytics Insight*, 30 Aug. 2022, www.analyticsinsight.net/5-ways-technology-has-improved-investments/. Accessed 2 Sept. 2023.

VNQ-Vanguard Real Estate ETF | Vanguard. (n.d.). https://investor.vanguard.com/investment-products/etfs/profile/vnq

Made in the USA
Columbia, SC
23 July 2024